THE HOME UNIVERSITY LIBRARY
OF MODERN KNOWLEDGE

228

WORLD HISTORY
FROM 1914 TO 1950

World History
from 1914 to 1950

DAVID THOMSON, PH.D.

Fellow of Sidney Sussex College and
Lecturer in History in the University of Cambridge

LONDON
OXFORD UNIVERSITY PRESS
NEW YORK TORONTO

*Oxford University Press, Amen House, London E.C.*4

GLASGOW   NEW YORK   TORONTO   MELBOURNE   WELLINGTON
BOMBAY   CALCUTTA   MADRAS   KARACHI   KUALA LUMPUR
CAPE TOWN   IBADAN   NAIROBI   ACCRA

First edition 1954
Reprinted 1958

PRINTED IN GREAT BRITAIN

FOR ALAN AND ROBERT

who may one day know
the second half of
the story

FOREWORD

THIS book has been written on two main assumptions. One is that a history of the world, in any period, need concern itself only with those events, movements, men, and ideas which have importance for the course of 'world history'. It is, therefore, no part of its purpose to give a continuous account of the history of any one nation, or even of any continent, between 1914 and 1950. Other works on a larger and more appropriate scale have done that already; and in the Introduction I have given reasons for supposing that, in this period, a collection of the separate and continuous histories of the six continents would not be 'world history' at all. The second assumption has been that the world historian ought to keep his feet on the earth. I have not conceived the purpose of contemporary history to be to serve as a finger of Providence, pointing towards some desirable or ineluctable solution for contemporary problems; and I have tried to avoid the occupational disease liable to afflict many writers on world affairs, which leads to indulgence in poetic imagery and intoxication with cosmic processes. Somewhere between safe generalizations about what has happened and very unsafe generalizations about why it has happened, there is perhaps room for generalizations about how it happened. This I have taken as my second test of relevance. But I know that it is only moderately safe, and in conjunction with my first test of relevance has led to the exclusion of much that some may reasonably expect to find in a book bearing this title. I can only hope and ask that readers will regard the result as I have regarded it: as one experiment in how recent world history can be written, a concrete example being usually more useful than a theoretical disquisition or a book of instructions.

Because maps of appropriate number and scale could not be included in a book of this kind and price, it has been decided to include none. But to consult a good atlas during the reading of it will considerably illuminate its arguments.

For the compilation of the index I am much indebted to the ingenuity and patience of Miss Kathleen Batchelor.

I would like to record my personal gratitude to the Provost of Oriel, Sir George Clark, for his kindness in reading the typescript with great care and making many valuable suggestions; and to both the Provost and Mr. Geoffrey Cumberlege for inviting me to undertake a task which has given me so much enjoyment. The fact that it has been written partly in England and partly in New York has, I hope, added something to its intercontinental approach.

D.T.

Sidney Sussex College,
Cambridge.
October 1953.

CONTENTS

INTRODUCTION

WHAT IS 'WORLD HISTORY'?

An attempt to deal, in one small book, with the last generation of world history needs some explanation, and perhaps some justification. It is possible because the concept of world history, as applied to the generation of mankind between 1914 and 1950, has a much more precise meaning than it can have when applied to any earlier generation: and this is not merely because it is the generation which has known two world wars.

Until some two hundred years ago even the most momentous events in one part of the world had very slight and remote repercussions, if they had any effects at all, in other parts of the world. Even the greatest upheavals in European history had no significance at all for the history of Australasia, little for Africa or Asia, and often only indirect significance for the history of North or South America. The fate of the six continents was not interlocked as it is interlocked to-day. It was 1788 before the first English settlement took place in Australia; it was 1853 before the American, Commodore Perry, compelled Japan to end her two centuries of seclusion from the rest of the world; it is only during the last hundred years that European power in Africa has penetrated beyond the frontier outposts and coastal strips into the vast interior.

It was therefore natural and proper, until recent

times, to regard the history of the world as consisting of separate accounts of each continent. Except for periodic irruptions of Asiatics into Europe, or of Europeans into North Africa or America, the development of each continent was a separate story. These irruptions might, in themselves, have drastic and far-reaching consequences: as did the barbarian invasions of Europe, or the Moslem invasions of Spain, or the Spanish conquests in South America. But even the total effect of these great movements was not to create a permanent and constant interaction between developments in each continent. Such an effect is the creation of only the last two centuries of modern history: only they constitute truly 'world history'. One feature of recent history is the spread of European power and influence throughout the world, and the manifold consequences of this both for Europe and for the other five continents. The result to-day is a world in which any momentous event anywhere really matters, within a relatively short time, to all other parts of the world: and the time within which it matters tends to get shorter. A revolution in Russia becomes of immediate and permanent concern to the rest of the earth; an economic depression in the United States affects the standards of living and rocks the political systems of most European nations; a war, breaking out initially between groups of nations in Europe, tends to spread until it entangles nearly every other people on the globe. It has become possible, therefore, for the historian of world history not to write the history of the continents separately. It is, indeed, no longer adequate for him to do so: and he must re-define the very concept of world history if he is to write it more adequately.

The historian of France does not write separate histories of Brittany, Provence, Burgundy and the rest of the French provinces, and then try to fit them together to compose a history of France. No historian does this because his horizon, his theme, his criterion of relevance and of significance, are necessarily different according to whether he is writing a history of the part or a history of the whole. National history and local history are subtly and intricately connected and interwoven, and study of one usually illuminates the other. But a collection of local histories cannot constitute a national history because the history of a nation is something other than the mere aggregate of the histories of all its several parts.

Likewise the history of a church or of a trade union is not the aggregate of the biographies of all its members. The biographies of trade unionists or of churchmen are relevant to the history of the institutions to which they belong only in so far as they have bearing on the over-all, long-term development of the institutions. In the same way, the histories of provinces and regions concern the historian of the nation only so far as they interlock with one another to constitute a significant element in the development of the nation as a whole. And although the conception even of European history has been less fully developed than it might be, it is generally recognized, tacitly in practice if not always explicitly in theory, that the historian of Europe is less concerned with an exhaustive compilation of separate national histories than with their periods of interaction and fusion into larger movements and developments. He deals not with the continuous history of Switzerland, Sweden or the Netherlands, but only with those periods in the history of these countries when they contributed something of general importance to the broader course of European civilization, or when they became a focus of international concern for the other nations of Europe. If he deals more continuously with the history of France or Germany, it is because these nations have exerted a more continuous influence on the general course of European history.

Yet this well recognized technique of the historian has, so far, been hardly at all applied to the history of the world. Separate nations, or geographical regions, or empires, or continents, or civilizations are studied, and their separate histories are written. Then these separate histories are joined end-to-end, as if this constituted a history of the world. Cross-references and chapters on international relations are added, in a vain attempt to complete the picture: vain, because there is no picture there to complete. The very concept of world history needs to be re-defined before a more adequate attempt to write it can even begin.

What has made a more coherent and precise concept of world history both possible and desirable in the present century is the modern interdependence of the continents. But this concept of interdependence, in turn, needs more careful definition. Many writers of the last generation, and most notably Mr H. G. Wells, urged the erection of world organization, both political and economic, on the grounds that the world was already materially one. In their enthusiasm for world integration they usually exaggerated the degree to which the peoples of the world are, even now, interdependent. The strength of isolationist, autarkic and separatist forces has been at least as much a feature of world history during the last fifty years as has the growth of international co-operation; and amidst more persistent efforts than ever before to achieve international order and harmony, the forces of separation have conquered new fields in Asia and Africa, and remain the strongest political forces at work in the modern world. These undeniable facts are warning enough against accepting, as the optimistic theme of modern history, the progressive unification of the world. Our grandchildren may see, in retrospect, an underlying explanation for the phenomena which we at present see only as irrepressible conflicts. They may come to regard both autarkic nationalism and international co-operation as equally manifestations of an underlying yearning for national or individual security. But we at least can see that, whatever may be the ultimate consequences, there has come about a situation which is novel in the history of the world. The essence of it is that, for the first time, the six continents of the world really matter to one another. For at least a good time to come bad harvests or economic depressions in any one of them will affect all the others; political revolutions or operative ideals in any one of them are a matter of immediate and intimate concern to all the others; and a war beginning anywhere can soon become a war which is happening everywhere. In this sense they are interdependent as they have never been before. It is interdependence in this sense, this perpetual interaction of one part of the world on all the other parts, which is the central theme of world history during the last fifty years. To explain how it has come about, what have been its main manifestations, and what have so far been its major consequences for mankind, is the essential task of the historian of world history since 1914. It is the task which this little book, tentatively and provisionally, attempts.

If this is accepted as the central theme and the main criterion of selection and relevance for the historian of world history since 1914, the history which he writes must resemble those maps of ocean-currents which show a flow of movement between continents, rather than those which show only the physical features of the separate continents. He must concern himself with the transformation of material conditions brought about by developments in science and technology, economic and social organization, world trade and investment. He must attempt a description and an analysis of this transformation such as will bring out its world-wide significance, and its inter-relation with political and cultural changes. The techniques and organizations of modern warfare have their place in this analysis, since the period concerned includes two world wars: indeed, they loom so large in the whole story that it is almost inevitable that he should view the period as falling into phases of pre-war, war and post-war conditions. Likewise, he must study international relations as an important aspect of this transformation. The history of war and peace, of diplomatic arrangements, of international and inter-continental migration, trade and investment, of organization designed to facilitate international co-operation, are all part of the same intricate story.

He must, secondly, concern himself with those general movements of ideas and human emotions which, though assuming local colouring in various parts of the world, are yet supranational and inter-continental in their meaning and importance. Movements such as nationalism and socialism, which originated long before 1914, have spread to new parts of the world since 1914, particularly to Asia and Africa. They have changed their character in so spreading. Communism and fascism, in diverse forms, have penetrated Europe and parts of Asia, Africa and America. The ideals of social security, economic democracy, and the welfare state have become concepts which have a world-wide significance.

He must, thirdly, concern himself with those persons who have become, in the popular phrase, 'world figures': men like Lenin and Gandhi, Woodrow Wilson and Franklin Roosevelt, Freud and Einstein, Bergson and Rutherford, Keynes and Beveridge. These men and their ideas and achievements have a place in the whole story which far transcends their roots in national soil. Even world figures long dead have some place, if their influence is still a live and operative force in shaping the history of the world. Christ and Mahomet, Marx and Darwin, are of direct relevance, because their

B

gospels and their ideas condition relations between men and peoples to-day.

Finally, and above all, he must concern himself with those events since 1914 which especially illuminate the interactions and inter-relations of all these other forces. The events of the two world wars, the process by which the League of Nations as a world organization broke down and by which the world schism between the Soviet and American Unions came about after 1945, the event of the dropping of the atomic bomb, are all integral parts of one story.

These four major concerns—material conditions, ideas and emotions, influential personalities and momentous events—are in a sense the basic categories of all historical analysis, and in the process of their interaction lies the secret of historical change. In this respect the method of the historian of the world is not ultimately different from the method of other historians. He is applying the familiar techniques of the modern historian on a spherical scale, and has to keep reminding himself that the world, being a globe, has no edges. The focus of his story is not this or that nation or continent: it is 'the great globe itself'.

The generation of mankind between 1914 and 1950, with which this book is concerned, belongs then to the phase of history to which this concept of world history is most completely applicable. To study the history of this generation is to study the most advanced phase of growing interdependence. But to study contemporary history is in itself subject to peculiar difficulties. Robbed of the historian's usual assets of hindsight, of knowing what in fact happened afterwards, the student of contemporary history is apt to find it more than usually difficult to see the wood for the trees. The difficulty is not, as is commmonly supposed, that the contemporary historian suffers from any scarcity of material or of factual knowledge. His handicap is the opposite—such superabundance of material with which to work that it is beyond the capacities of any one individual to master it all. It is not true that 'we do not yet know enough about recent events'. We know a great deal more about the Battle of Britain than about the Battle of Hastings. The difficulty is that whereas, for the historian of the Battle of Hastings, the evidence has been arbitrarily diminished in quantity by the hazards of time, the evidence about the Battle of Britain has remained so vast and so unravaged by time that its historian has to find for himself a principle of selection and of abridgement which will enable him to reduce it to manageable proportions. It is difficult to see why, as is often suggested, the result should be less objective or less accurate than the result of the researches of the medieval historian. The account built up by the cautious contemporary historian is, indeed, much less likely to be substantially changed by the discovery of hitherto unknown facts than is that of the medieval historian. He has far richer means of checking each of his statements than has his medieval colleague, and he might even be expected to build a more solid and durable account.

But the contemporary historian's chief difficulty is to ensure some detachment and perspective, and due

proportion in interpreting his subject. It is here that the
student of world history, in the sense described above,
may have an especially valuable contribution to make
to the study of contemporary history. The chief distortions of contemporary history come from the limitations
of nationality. All national historians are, from the
point of view of world history, prone to parochialism.
Just because nationalism remains one of the strongest
forces in the modern world, it is almost impossible for
the contemporary historian to escape its inhibiting
parochialism. But it may be expected that the more he
strives to view all national histories from a supra-
national and international standpoint, the more he will
be able to free himself from such distortions. In this
sense it can be argued that the study of world history is
the necessary accompaniment to the study of contemporary history. It is not only that true world history is,
of necessity, recent history: it is also that recent history
can be adequately studied only as world history.

· · · · ·

The realities behind the two portmanteau words
'nationalism' and 'socialism', which have been used at
several points in the book, are easier to describe or to
recognize than to define. But it should be added that a
nation has been taken to mean a community of people
whose sense of belonging together derives from their
belief that they have a common homeland and from experience of common traditions and historical development: and nationalism usually means the desire of such
a community to assert its unity and independence

vis-à-vis other communities or groups. Socialism, despite a variety of usages, has been here taken to mean the belief that human society should be so organized that the modes of producing and distributing wealth will serve the primary needs of all members of the society before the secondary needs of any members are satisfied. It thus differs fundamentally from communism which, in its only significant contemporary forms of Marxism, Leninism, Stalinism, and Trotskyism, seeks first to 'liquidate the bourgeoisie' by revolutionary and therefore violent means and so to deny even the primary needs of those members of the society on whom the ruling party can affix the label 'bourgeois'. Neither the word 'nationalism' nor the word 'socialism' has been used as a term of approbation or of abuse, but simply as terms descriptive of undeniably important phenomena in the modern world.

Chapter One

THE WORLD SCENE IN 1914

§1. *The Political Setting*

THE surface of the earth consists of more than 55 million square miles of land and more than 141 million square miles of water. In 1914 the population of the world was probably some 1,800 million souls. Roughly one-quarter of this number lived in Europe, and well over half in Asia: so the centre of gravity of mankind lay in Eurasia. In 1914 the British Commonwealth[1] covered a quarter of the surface of the earth and included about a quarter of mankind. But its population was very unevenly distributed, and compared with the concentration of people in Eurasia it was peripheral. Most of it, indeed, lived in the densely populated areas of India and the British Isles; but the rest was scattered over Africa, Canada, Australasia, and many small islands and outposts. Through its naval power the Commonwealth had control over most of the seas, and because of its peripheral character this power was crucial to its whole economic and political structure. It also owned nearly half the world's tonnage of merchant shipping. This territorial and demographic distribution of the Commonwealth, combined with its naval and

---

[1] It would be technically more correct to speak of the 'British Empire' before 1922, then of the 'British Commonwealth and Empire' until 1947, and since then of the 'Commonwealth of Nations'. To avoid clumsiness and confusion the words 'British Commonwealth' or 'Commonwealth' have been used throughout.

commercial strength, made it one of the main links between the six continents, and perhaps the greatest single
factor making for their political interdependence. In
1950 it was still the only completely inter-continental
power in the world.

The territories of the Commonwealth mostly fell
into two groups: those which bordered the shores of the
North Atlantic and those which surrounded the Indian
Ocean. The main exceptions were the West African
territories on the shores of the South Atlantic; small
but important outposts, such as Gibraltar, Malta, and
Cyprus, in the Mediterranean; and others, such as
Hong Kong and Singapore, in the Far East. British
naval power could, therefore, be mainly concentrated
in the North Atlantic and the Indian Ocean, whilst
using the intermediate islands and bases as links between these areas of concentration. But diplomatically
Britain was inevitably interested in any important
political events anywhere in Europe, Africa, North
America, the Indian Ocean and the Far East. For this
reason she found herself, by 1914, in acute rivalry with
Germany, which was challenging her naval supremacy
in the Atlantic and North Sea; in close understanding
with France, since 1904, about North Africa, the
Mediterranean and the North Sea; and in alliance with
Japan, since 1902, and with Russia, since 1907. As
France and Russia had also, since 1894, been in alliance
against possible attack by Germany and her allies,
Britain found herself a partner in a 'Triple Entente'
against the common menace of Germany. Secure in the
Far East because of her agreements with Japan and

Russia, she could concentrate her main attention on Europe and the bulk of her naval power in the waters of the North Atlantic and the North Sea.

In any survey of the world scene in 1914 it is necessary to put the British Commonwealth in the forefront, simply because it was the largest and most obviously world-wide power. It was also the most conspicuous and most successful product of a phase of world history which was already coming to an end: the colonial expansion of the European powers. This phase reached an end with the final partition of Africa, marked by the creation of the Union of South Africa as a Dominion of the British Commonwealth in 1910. During the scramble for Africa Britain had come into rivalry with most of her western European neighbours: but by 1914 colonial rivalries of this kind were receding. Since 1904 Britain had come to terms with her chief colonial rival, France, by agreeing to French hegemony in Morocco in exchange for French recognition of British hegemony in Egypt and in the Anglo-Egyptian Sudan. The French and British colonies in Africa lay side by side, and both were now firmly delimited. French Africa covered an area of more than 4 million square miles, with some 30 million inhabitants. It included most of the North African coast (Tunisia and Algeria, with control over Morocco), French West Africa, and the Congo. British West Africa included Gambia, Sierra Leone, the Gold Coast, and Nigeria. Interspersed with these French and British colonies were those of the other western European maritime nations. Portugal held a small coastal area of Guinea and the large area of Angola. Spain held part of Morocco and Rio de Oro in West Africa, as well as the Canary Islands. Belgium had the vast internal area of the Congo, which she had annexed by 1907. Germany had the Cameroons, Togoland and South-West Africa. Italy, as recently as 1912, had gained Libya from Turkey. In this way the whole of the Mediterranean and West African coastlines, with their hinterlands, were parcelled out among the western European maritime nations.

This was the position on the eastern shores of the Atlantic. What of its western shores? Here the Monroe Doctrine of the United States had, for nearly a century, aimed at preserving the American continent from corresponding intervention by the European powers in American affairs. The partition of Africa, which had mainly happened during the generation before 1914, had strengthened the United States in its determination to keep the old world from upsetting the balance of the new. Britain was firmly established in Canada, in the British West Indies, in British Honduras in Central America, and in British Guiana in South America. The French had also a part of Guiana, and a few tiny North Atlantic islands such as Saint-Pierre and Miquelon. But since 1898 other European powers had been without any foothold in America. In that year war with Spain had given the United States a large measure of control over the Caribbean. The island of Cuba, even after a grant of formal independence in 1901, remained under United States protection. Puerto Rico was taken under direct control. President Theodore Roosevelt and his successors had sent American troops or warships to Santo Domingo, Haiti, Colombia, Mexico, and Nicaragua to squash revolutions, control finances, or preserve a government favourable to United States interests. The first International American Conference met at Washington in 1889, and out of it grew the Pan American Union which held three more conferences between 1901 and 1910. When world war broke out, United States troops were engaged in Mexico, overthrowing a revolutionary government and asserting American interests; and they were not finally withdrawn until 1916.

In this way the trend of political events by 1914 in the Atlantic was towards a consolidated grip by the western European nations on the eastern Atlantic shores, but their elimination from any serious influence over the western shores; and their replacement, in South America, by the United States as the predominant external influence. The single great exception was the British Dominion of Canada. Here there was a powerful trend towards the assertion of greater Canadian independence from Britain, as well as from the United States. Under the premiership of Sir Robert Borden, even more than under his Liberal predecessor Laurier, Canadian nationalism took the political form of combining loyalty to the Commonwealth with a vigorous assertion of the right to shape any foreign policy which might involve Canadian forces. Canadians feared that Britain might be tempted to sacrifice Canadian interests in order to win United States support. These fears had been stimulated by the British handling of the Alaska boundary dispute of 1903, when the boundary was fixed mainly in favour of the United States. Ever since the unhappy and hysterical behaviour of President Cleveland towards Britain's dispute with Venezuela in 1895, British policy had been to harmonize the interests of the two major North Atlantic nations. On that occasion a petty dispute about the boundary between British Guiana and Venezuela evoked an excitable reassertion of the Monroe Doctrine which, for a few weeks, brought Britain and the United States to the brink of war. The affair cleared the air between the two countries, increased their mutual respect, and opened their eyes to the dangers of intransigence on either side. From 1906 the British Navy was redistributed in three main fleets, in the eastern Atlantic, the Channel, and the Mediterranean.[1] The squadron hitherto based on Bermuda to cover the British West Indies was withdrawn. It left the United States with a free hand in the Caribbean, and marked a truce to any naval rivalry between Britain and the U.S.A.

. . . . .

In the other major sphere of British interests, the Indian Ocean, there was a similar intermingling of the colonial territories of the European maritime powers. On the east of Africa, as on the west, they had partitioned the coastline. There were Italian Somaliland, French Somaliland, and British Somaliland: Portuguese East Africa, German East Africa, and British East

---

[1] Within the next few years naval arrangements with France concentrated British commitments in the North Sea and Channel, in return for French co-operation in naval defence of the Mediterranean.

Africa. In addition, Italy held Eritrea, France the island of Madagascar, and Britain Rhodesia and Uganda. The only remaining states of the whole African continent with any degree of independence, apart from the Union of South Africa itself, were Egypt, Abyssinia, and Liberia. On the northern shores of the Indian Ocean lay the vast British territories of India and Burma, with the island of Ceylon. On the eastern shores lay the Federated Malay States, with the key naval base of Singapore as Britain's vital link between the Indian Ocean and the Pacific; the rich chain of the Dutch East Indies; and to the south Australasia. Here the United States exerted no direct influence and held no territories. Most of the many small islands scattered over the Indian Ocean were in British control. It was, even more obviously than the eastern Atlantic, a British sea. The chief emigrants within its shores were the Indians. After slavery had been abolished within the British Empire in 1833 a demand had grown up for labour in tropical areas, and this led to the emigration of Indians on indenture. The system was coming to an end by 1914, but many Indians stayed on in their adopted countries, such as Mauritius or the Union of South Africa.

The links between the Atlantic and Indian Oceans, as twin areas of British interests and influence, were on the one hand the long sea-route round the Cape of Good Hope, which was also in British hands; and on the other, since the Suez Canal had been built in 1869, there was the much shorter route through the Mediterranean and the Red Sea. With Gibraltar and Malta in

British control, the island of Cyprus added since 1878, Aden occupied since 1839, and a large share of control over the Suez Canal since 1875, communications between Britain and the Indian Ocean seemed assured. Despite this intermixture of colonial territories and interests along all three sides of the great geographical triangle of Africa, all substantial disputes had been settled by 1914, so far as the scramble for Africa was concerned. Germany and Italy, having achieved political unification only within the previous fifty years, had come late into the field of colonial scramble. They had a more meagre share and a less attractive colonial empire than most of their western European neighbours. But it was unlikely that any African animosities remaining by 1914 would, in themselves, embroil these powers in war with one another.

.   .   .   .   .

In the Pacific and the Far East there was a different balance of imperial forces. There, too, the British Commonwealth was involved. In the southern Pacific it was represented by Australia, New Zealand and Tasmania, the Fiji and Solomon Islands, and other lesser territories. On the west it had part of New Guinea and North Borneo. But in the northern Pacific it was Japan which was the expansionist power. She was expanding mainly at the expense of China, which she defeated in war in 1894-5. The western powers, too, sought ports and concessions which would open up to them the vast resources and markets of China. Russia, Germany, France and Britain, as well as Japan, had planted

themselves at various strategic points on her coastline.
It seemed like the story of the partition of Africa all
over again. For seventy-two years Britain had held the
crucial port of Hong Kong, at the mouth of the Canton
River, and she had developed it into the most important commercial centre in China. In 1871 Russia had
seized the province of Kulja. In Indo-China French
protectorates had been established over Cambodia
since 1863, over Tonkin since 1883, over Annam since
1884, and over Laos since 1893. Cochin-China was
ceded to her in 1868. Britain, in 1886, had annexed
Burma. As a result of her war with China, Japan gained
control over Korea and annexed it in 1910; and would
have got a good deal of Manchuria too had not Russia,
Germany and France restrained her by protests. Between 1895 and 1900 all the powers competed for concessions and 'spheres of influence' in China, building
railways and granting loans. These intrusions fostered
a wave of something akin to nationalism in China, and
led to the Boxer rebellion at Pekin in 1900. Japan,
Russia, France, Britain, and eventually Germany sent
a joint force to suppress it, and in the same year Britain
and Germany signed a convention by which they
agreed to restrain foreign territorial aggression in
China, and maintain the 'open door' for world trade.
The year before, the United States, too, had come into
the picture. Her Secretary of State, John Hay, supported the doctrine of the open door, in the sense that
powers holding concessions in China were expected
not to discriminate against others by differential tariffs
or railway rates. It did nothing to protect China from

such penetrations, but it did ameliorate the rivalries of the great powers.

In 1904 war broke out between Russia and Japan, and in the following year President Theodore Roosevelt used his good offices to bring it to an end. But it left Japan in a more favourable position than Russia to exploit China's weakness. In 1911 the declining Manchu dynasty in China was overthrown. It had ruled the country since 1644, and now a republic was set up. Dr Sun Yat-sen and his nationalist party, the Kuomintang, succeeded in establishing their authority only in the south at Canton. In the north power fell to the military governors of the different provinces, who established themselves as independent and quarrelsome war-lords. This unstable position, which existed in 1914, was clearly unlikely to last. It indicated that China would become a future focus of world tension.

Only in the twentieth century did the United States become as interested in the Pacific as she was in the Atlantic. The making of the Panama Canal, which by 1914 was incomplete but open to traffic, gave her a direct sea-route between the two main theatres of her national interest comparable to the link which the opening of the Suez Canal, a generation earlier, had provided for the British Commonwealth. Her increasing political interest in the Pacific came mainly from her acquisition of Guam and the Philippines as a result of the Spanish-American War: but her willing acceptance of these advanced naval bases in the Far East was, in turn, due to her already increasing economic and naval interest in that area. Hawaii and part of Samoa were acquired at about the same time. Thus the war which ejected the last European power from the New World also gave the United States a more positive link with the Far East. This brought new factors into her foreign policy. So far as the Atlantic was concerned, her main aim was to prevent the intrusion of Europe into American affairs. In the Far East the presence of European powers could be neither denied nor ignored, and it was impossible to adopt so negative and defensive an attitude. John Hay's 'open door' policy of 1899 was the result of pressure from manufacturing and trading interests for a firmer policy, and from certain missionary groups. Lord Charles Beresford's book *The Break-up of China* was timely and sensational, whilst Admiral Mahan's works reminded Americans of the importance of sea power. It was a period of imperial expansion overseas for America, corresponding to the African and Far Eastern expansion of the European powers. Once drawn into the Far East, the crucial problem for America was inevitably China. The United States took her place amongst the mercantile nations of the world watching, with some anxiety, the imminent break-up of that country.

.   .   .   .

These entanglements of the European powers overseas were, however, very much less inflammable than their rivalries within the continent of Europe itself. It is here that the deepest roots of the first world war can be found. Whilst new maritime empires were being built up by the western powers overseas, older continental dynastic empires were breaking up in Eurasia. The roots of the trouble in Europe were the consequences of the crumbling of the dual Habsburg monarchy of Austria-Hungary, the sprawling Turkish empire of the Ottomans, and the vast Russian empire of the Romanovs. The forces of nationalism and liberalism, which had been fermenting in the rest of Europe for over a century, had only recently begun to have their full impact on these multi-national and non-national dynastic conglomerations. Already there had been stirrings of revolt in Poland, partitioned for so long between Austria-Hungary, Russia, and Prussia; already the Greeks and some of the southern Slavs had broken away from their Habsburg or Ottoman rulers; and Turkey had for long been regarded as 'the sick man of Europe'.

Turkey was disintegrating faster than Austria-Hungary: but the position of the latter was more dangerous, because of the powerful challenge to her very survival offered by the aggressive and highly nationalistic Balkan state of Serbia. An independent state for nearly a century, Serbia had recently gained both in size and strength, and was now backed by Russia in her Pan-Slav policy in eastern Europe. Russia, though beset internally by revolutionary stirrings which led to the experiments with the Duma in 1905, was in a position to take the offensive on behalf of other Slav nations in eastern Europe. When Turkey in 1912 was defeated by the Balkan states powerful impetus was given to the disintegration of the Ottoman Empire. Both Russia and Austria-Hungary had an eye on any

c

pickings that might come from that process. At the same time Germany, too, was evolving clear ambitions in the Near East, of which the Berlin-Bagdad Railway was the omen; Britain was interested in Persia, and in 1907 made an agreement with Russia by which Britain gained as a 'sphere of influence' the southern part of the country, Russia the northern part, with a neutral zone between them; France was particularly interested in Syria, where she had investments, Christian missions, and schools, and a desire to maintain and extend her Levantine interests. The Balkans and the Levant were also the meeting-point of that curious series of 'Pan' movements which appeared by the beginning of the century. In addition to Pan-Slavism, which was important only so far as it was a convenient agency of Russian expansionism, there were the Pan-German and Pan-Teutonic movements in reaction against Pan-Slavism, a Pan-Turanian movement which aspired to unite all branches of the Turkish race from Thrace to Siberia, and a Pan-Islam movement which stretched from North Africa to India. The increasing contacts between peoples, especially between peoples very different in civilization and race, had led to association of the concept of civilization with that of race. But movements for racial unification have been, in effect, little more than weapons of national domination, and this was as true of Pan-Slavism, Pan-Germanism, and Pan-Turanianism before 1914 as it was true of National Socialism in Germany between the wars.

The awakening of the Moslem world to a sense of unity was one of the most significant developments which took place at this time. The Moslem League in India, founded in 1907, was one sign of it. The division of Persia in the same year; the occupation of Morocco by the French; the attacks first of Italy, in 1911, and then of the Balkan States in 1912, on Turkey: these seemed to add up to a joint attack of the European nations on Islam, and gave great impetus to the Pan-Islam movement. It was to prove an important factor in world affairs at the end of the first world war. Meanwhile the Turkish government, like its counterpart in China, faced a nationalist revolt. In 1908 the Young Turks revolted in Salonika and demanded from the Sultan a constitution. He agreed, but straightway war broke out against the new dictators, and Europeans and Arabs alike helped to split up the Turkish Empire. Bulgaria declared her independence; Greece took Crete; Austria-Hungary took the provinces of Bosnia and Herzegovina; Italy took Tripoli; in Bagdad Iraqi nationalists demanded independence for Mesopotamia; in Damascus Syrian nationalists followed suit; in Nejd Ibn Saud claimed independence for Arabia. In such empires nationalism at the centre bred separatist nationalisms on the periphery. This example served to remind the governors of Austria-Hungary that they, too, were in peril of a similar fate should separatist nationalism grow in the Balkans.

This complex tangle of conflicting nationalisms and imperialisms in the Balkans and the Levant put great strain on the diplomatic system of alliances in Europe. Because Germany feared encirclement by the Triple Entente powers of Russia, France and Britain she dared not desert Austria-Hungary, which was now intent on demolishing the rising power of Serbia. Because France feared Germany, she dared not desert Russia, however much she might encourage Serbia to resist. Because Britain feared Germany's challenge to her naval supremacy, she dared not desert France. The alliances conspired to draw all separate issues together into one vast dispute.

The Triple Alliance of Germany, Austria-Hungary, and Italy had been forged between 1879, when Bismarck made his Dual Alliance with Austria-Hungary for defence against Russia, and 1882, when these two powers signed the Triple Alliance Treaty with Italy. Bismarck's constant aim after his defeat of France in 1870 had been to keep France isolated in Europe, and to prevent any diplomatic encirclement of Germany. The result had been to create, in effect, two rival systems of alliances, and to establish a delicate balance of power in Europe which, for a generation, helped to keep the peace. So long as one combination automatically prompted a rival counter-combination, so that an ultimate balance of power was maintained, both sides were restrained from breaking the peace. But recurrent tensions and prolonged rivalry of this kind in itself produced a constant competition in armaments, and bred ever more widespread fear which in the end pulled all the powers involved into one great war. Instead of the less interested and more cool-headed partners restraining their allies, fear became so universal in Europe that it was the more hot-headed and warlike partners who set the pace for their allies. No dispute could be limited or localized because each involved all the others. That is why the murder of the Austrian Archduke by a Serbian fanatic in the little Balkan town of Sarajevo set Russia and France at war with Austria-Hungary and Germany; and why the invasion of Belgium by Germany brought Britain and the British Dominions into the general conflict. Mr J. A. Spender summed up the European position well:

The stage which Europe had reached was that of a semi-internationalism which organized the nations into two groups but provided no bridge between them. There could scarcely have been worse conditions for either peace or war. The equilibrium was so delicate that a puff of wind might destroy it, and the immense forces on either side were so evenly balanced that a struggle between them was bound to be stupendous. The very success of the balance of power was in this respect its nemesis.[1]

Because of the world-wide colonial connexions of the great powers, the war which ensued was in a limited sense a 'world war'; but the empires of the Triple Alliance powers were so predominantly continental dynastic empires that major hostilities were soon confined to Europe, the Mediterranean, and the Atlantic. The Far East was concerned directly only in so far as Indian troops fought in the British forces. The German colonies in Africa were speedily isolated, though a long and costly campaign went on in German East Africa until 1918.

•   •   •   •   •   •

[1] J. A. Spender: *Fifty Years of Europe* (1933), p. 389.

The world scene in 1914, viewed as a whole, had as its most striking feature the impact of expansionist powers upon older and unresilient powers, with consequent repercussions upon relations between these expansionist powers themselves. This is the over-all pattern. Russia, Japan, Britain, Germany, France were impinging on China; Russia, Italy, Britain, France, and the Balkan States were impinging on the Ottoman Empire. In each case this impact stimulated a nationalist revolution, which in turn was accompanied by other separatist national revolts within these ancient empires. In Austria-Hungary the impact of Russia, Serbia, and the other Balkan States produced internal separatist movements but without a national revolution at the centre. British influence in India, and United States influence over South America, are comparable developments: as is the partition of the African continent amongst the European powers. Here the consequences of internal nationalist reactions have been slower to develop, but so far bear sufficient resemblance to the familiar pre-1914 pattern to have significance. In India the Morley-Minto reforms of 1909 conceded representative institutions on a very limited scale. The Indian National Congress, dating from 1885, was by 1914 the main vehicle of Hindu nationalism: and the Moslem League was founded in 1907. Distinctive South American and African manifestations of nationalist revolt against foreign domination have appeared as important developments only since the first world war.

If this pattern provides an accurate general analysis of the political scene in the world of 1914, it should mean that the future would lie with those powers whose outlook, traditions, and ideals best fitted them to come to terms with these novel forces of nationalism. Two powers especially stood for the comprehension of a wide diversity of races and nationalities within a common framework of government and administration: the British Commonwealth and the United States. Four Dominions had recently gained almost complete self-government and national independence. With the addition of Saskatchewan and Alberta by 1905, the Dominion of Canada completed its federal unification. The Dominion of New Zealand, dating from 1852, was formally constituted in 1907. The Commonwealth of Australia was inaugurated in 1901. In 1910 the self-governing colonies of the Cape of Good Hope, Natal, the Transvaal, and the Orange River Colony combined to form the Union of South Africa. The twentieth century brought for the British Commonwealth not only completion of the development of the settled colonies towards full and responsible self-government, but also a process of internal unification and consolidation. This combined British with French settlers in Canada, British and Dutch in South Africa. The United States, by a comparable development, had found a means for comprising men and women of nearly every race, religion, and nationality within a common citizenship, and was producing from the mixture a new concept of distinctive American nationality.

The exceptions to this successful handling of nationalist difficulties without disruption were India and Ireland in the Commonwealth, and the negro in the United

States. In India, as in Ireland, the twin problems of self-government and national independence were cut across by the bitter strife of religious differences, and became connected with unsettling issues of territorial partition. In 1914 the Liberal Government of Mr Asquith was about to pass a Home Rule Bill which would coerce Ulster into accepting union with southern Ireland and separation from Great Britain, whilst the Unionist opposition supported Ulster separatism from southern Ireland as an obstacle to Home Rule. Only the coming of war postponed the issue, and within four years of the end of the war an inconclusive civil war in Ireland was to bring independence to southern Ireland but also partition between southern and northern Ireland. Between 1905 and 1911 the partition of Bengal raised a similar conflict between Hindu and Moslem in India: and a generation later Indian independence, too, was to be attained only at the price of partition. The position of the negro in the United States, which had also in the past helped to bring about civil war and the threat of partition, was America's biggest failure to absorb all comers. Negroes were given the vote in 1870, but remained the least completely absorbed of all elements in the great 'melting-pot' of races.

Both countries were confronted with the problem of how much further they could extend these principles of liberal grants of self-government and political independence to formerly dependent peoples, without incurring separatism or partition. How far could Britain extend Dominion status to India, to Burma and Ceylon, to her major African colonies? How far could the United

States encourage self-government in Cuba, or in the Philippines? These problems remained to be tackled during the post-war years. Meanwhile, it seemed, dynastic empires which rested on the denial or the subjugation of nationalist aspirations were doomed to disintegration. It seems reasonably certain that both these developments would have taken place even had there been no world war. What the war did was to hasten and facilitate both.

§2. *The Economic Stage*

During the nineteenth century some 40 million emigrants left Europe and some 9 million Chinese left China to go overseas. The Europeans went mainly to America and Australasia, the Chinese partly to these but mainly to the tropical fringe of Asia. A considerable proportion, impossible to estimate accurately, had returned home, either because they had always meant to or because they had failed to establish and adapt themselves to their new environment. The flow of emigrants from Europe was just reaching its height in 1914. Between 1906 and 1910 the annual average had become 1,400,000. At the same time there took place an eastern migration of Russians into Asiatic Russia from European Russia, whose population increased by half between 1890 and 1914. During the nineteenth century some 3,700,000 had gone, and between 1900 and 1914 another 3,500,000 followed. This remarkable movement of peoples out of Europe and out of China helped to populate the peripheral countries of the globe. It did nothing to depopulate Eurasia as a whole, which was

growing in total numbers. It was encouraged by the
growth of rapid and cheap transport, by railway and
steamship, during the second half of the nineteenth
century. A revolution in means of transport and communication was already transforming relations between
the continents of the world.

By 1914, over 516,000 kilometres of cables had been
laid on the ocean beds, and networks of telegraph and
telephone lines covered the world. In the previous
generation the whole world, save the most remote corners, had been reduced for economic purposes to one
market, with news of prices, supplies, and demands so
rapid. Over 30,000 ships, with a total tonnage of nearly
50 million tons, carried the world's sea-borne traffic;
and nearly half of them belonged to the British Commonwealth. The world's chief ship-builder was the
United Kingdom, which built more ships than all the
world's other ship-yards put together. As she tended to
sell her older ships and build newer types for herself,
the British merchant marine was not only the largest
but also the most up-to-date and efficient. Communications between continents by steamships had been
extended across continents by railways. The first
United States transcontinental railway was opened in
1869, the Canadian Pacific Railway was completed by
1885, and the Trans-Caucasian and Siberian Railways
by 1905. The opening of the Suez Canal in 1869 and of
the Panama Canal in 1914 created continuous and
shorter sea-routes between the Mediterranean and the
Indian Ocean, and between the Atlantic and the Pacific.
The North Sea and Baltic were likewise linked by the

Kiel Canal, open since 1895 but reconstructed in 1914. Never before had it been so easy, cheap or quick to move men or goods from one part of the globe to another.

Yet all these developments, and this new mobility of men and materials, did not have the more cohesive effects which might be expected and which have often been claimed. The revolution in transportation and communication combined with other political trends and other economic developments to produce a medley of different effects, some unifying and some disintegrating. What it essentially did was to change the balance of economic advantages, sometimes offsetting former disadvantages and sometimes reinforcing previous advantages. The natural advantage which Great Britain had formerly enjoyed as an industrial power, in having her iron and coal resources close to one another, was now offset in both the United States and Germany by the introduction of cheap railroad transport. This made it economically profitable to bring together the ores of Lake Superior and the coal of Pittsburg, to make steel; or to transport coal to Belgium, Holland, Denmark, and Russia by railroad from Germany rather than by sea from Great Britain. On the other hand, the strategic maritime position of the British Isles, which had made them so natural a commercial centre, was now reinforced by the development of transatlantic steamship lines. The fact that the United States was just reaching the point where she had a surplus of manufactures for export after satisfying the needs of her vast domestic market, whereas Germany had reached that point a generation sooner, made the United States—despite her much greater resources and production—appear to British eyes less of a rival than Germany.

It was the building of the whole railway network in Europe, combined with the political unification of Germany after 1871, which gave Germany great new commercial advantages hitherto enjoyed by Britain. Professor L. C. A. Knowles put it well:

Hindered hitherto by a short coast line, by the Northern flow of her rivers and by the freezing of her canals in winter, she gained new outlets East, West and South at all times of the year. She became a Mediterranean power by the completion of the railway over the St. Gotthard in 1882. She obtained great economic influence in Northern Italy and Genoa became an important German outlet. In the same way the railway to Constantinople made her a power in the Balkans with commercial interests in the Levant. She was connected by railway with France on the West and Russia on the East and became the centre of the continental system of distribution, thereby affecting the hitherto unrivalled sea distributing position of England.[1]

These changes are symptomatic of a whole series of shifts in the economic balance of the world which were already being brought about by the growth of mechanical transport. A decade before war broke out the three countries had a foreign trade the comparative value of which is indicated by the following figures. They show the preponderance of the United States in exports of all kinds, but the preponderance of the United Kingdom

[1] L. C. A. Knowles: *The Industrial and Commercial Revolutions in Great Britain during the Nineteenth Century* (1921), p. 187.

in export of manufactured goods, and as a customer in world markets for raw materials. They also show how Germany was her more important rival as a producer of manufactured goods.

Annual average, 1900-1904	£ Million		
	U.S.A.	Germany	U.K.
Exports—total	292.3	235.6	282.7
Exports—manufactured goods only	99.8	154.2	224.7
Imports—total	186.0	287.0	466.0
Imports—manufactured goods only	78.6	57.0	113.4

The emergence of the United States as a great exporting nation explains her new and lively interest in world affairs by 1900. British exports went almost as much to Europe as to the countries of the British Commonwealth: though nearly two-thirds of India's imports came from the United Kingdom alone, and constituted over 13 per cent. of the total exports of the United Kingdom.[1]

A further index of the relative commercial strengths of the leading industrial nations is their mercantile tonnage of shipping. In June, 1914, the figures for vessels

[1] One third of the United Kingdom's exports went to European countries, including Russia: just over 37 per cent. went to countries of the British Commonwealth.

of 100 tons or over were: United States 5.4 million tons; Germany 5.5 million tons; United Kingdom 19.3 million tons; British Commonwealth as a whole 21.1 million tons. Here Britain held her nineteenth-century supremacy by a long lead, but ten years later the United States proportion had risen to a quarter of the total, whilst the United Kingdom's had dropped to 30 per cent. of the total: and this tendency was already apparent even before the war brought heavy losses to Britain and a tremendous boom to shipbuilding in the United States.

In this general shift of balance in commercial and industrial power, France suffered even more than Great Britain. Between 1870 and 1904 the output of her blast-furnaces had increased sixfold, but Germany's increased tenfold. In 1904, when Germany's total exports were worth £235.6 million, France's were worth only £168.6 million. Whereas Germany's mercantile shipping, in 1914, was 5.5 million tons, France's was only 2.3 million tons. The level of her population was barely maintained, even with large-scale immigration, which came mainly from Belgium, Italy, and Germany. Although some immigration was only temporary, there were from 1872 to 1911 nearly a million naturalizations, mainly under an act of 1889 which made naturalization easier; and there were still, in 1911, 1,132,696 aliens reported to be living in France. Germany's population grew from 40 million in 1870 to 68 million by 1914.

Increased ease and decreased cost of movement might have been expected to lead to great migration. But because this technological development coincided with the raising of barriers against immigration, there tended to be actually less inter-continental migration in the twentieth century than there was during the nineteenth. The Chinese were excluded from the United States after 1882, from Hawaii after 1898, from the Philippines after 1902. The United States excluded Japanese labourers in 1907, and by the Immigration Act of 1917 barred the entry of other non-Europeans, especially Indians and inhabitants of the East Indies. Canada took similar action against the Chinese after 1885, and against the Japanese after 1908. New Zealand restricted Chinese, and Australia passed a federal Immigration Restriction Act in 1901, with the same purpose. The Union of South Africa barred Chinese in 1913. Some of the South American States followed suit, but Argentina, Brazil, and Chile did not discriminate against non-Europeans, and Brazil even encouraged Japanese settlers. Before 1914 the United States and the British Dominions took little action to exclude European immigrants, although already literacy tests and preferences could in some countries be applied to Europeans. The main impediments to European migration came after the war.

Corresponding obstacles to the movement of goods were imposed by a growing network of tariff barriers and preferences. The age when Great Britain and the United States had stood for almost complete freedom of trade had passed. All countries were seeking to protect their manufactures or their trade by governmental controls, subsidies, and tariffs. The decade of Conservative Party government in Britain between 1895 and

1905 brought some demand to return to protectionism. Joseph Chamberlain's Tariff Reform League, demanding protection as a unifying force within the Empire, merged gradually into an anti-free trade movement, backed by manufacturers but wanting duties on imported food, with a preference for the colonies, and an average 10 per cent. tariff on foreign manufactured goods. But it made little headway before 1914. In the United States the McKinley tariff of 1890 was designed to be used as a bargaining card to gain privileges for American exports, and to a great measure it succeeded. The Dingley tariff, seven years later, raised duties higher than ever before, and in spite of the adjustments made by the Payne-Aldrich tariffs of 1909 and the Underwood tariff of 1913, the United States remained the most protectionist country in the world in 1914.

The leading industrial nations of Europe followed suit. France, traditionally a protectionist country, returned to her traditions with the Méline tariff of 1892, and in 1910 carried them further. Farmers and manufacturers made common cause in demanding protection, and by 1914 France was one of the most strictly protected countries in Europe. Germany was especially concerned to protect her agriculture and to promote her own heavy industries, and her tariffs of 1902 were designed to hold the balance between these two aims. Industrial expansion and exports were more important to her, economically, than a highly protected agriculture: but fear of war dictated that she pay some regard to her agricultural production. So the concessions she could make to other states were small, and she remained

—like the rest of central Europe—committed to a highly protective fiscal system. At the same time Russia, for quite different reasons, was erecting very high barriers. Her aim was to accumulate gold reserves in order to stabilize her currency; and, as she depended so much on foreign investments and loans, she was anxious that the interest in these should so far as possible be paid not in gold but in goods. Her chief export was corn. Her aim, therefore, was to erect such tariffs as would enable her to force down the duties of others on her exports of corn, and to cut down her imports of manufactured goods. The underlying aim was a self-contained empire, and it was the shadow of autarky to come. After a tariff war with Germany in the 1890s, she settled down to two decades of general protectionism.

By making the economy of each country more sensitive to changes elsewhere, the growth of world trade aroused new anxieties. These prompted immigration restrictions and tariff wars, just when the spread of industrialism and of world trade was making continents and countries more interdependent. By shifting the old balance of natural advantages, it bred new and more ferocious national rivalries. The British Isles, by their precocious and pioneer industrialization, had by 1914 become utterly dependent on world trade not only for maintaining their standard of living, but for their basic subsistence needs. Three-quarters of the corn Britain consumed came from overseas. Her best customer for manufactured goods was India, which took over 13 per cent. of Britain's exports. But both Germany and the United States were producing the very goods which had

D

been her chief exports—coal, iron and steel, and ships. Although still the largest exporter of coal, her average annual production of coal was already very much less than that of the United States:[1] and Germany was exporting nearly half as much coal as Britain, even though she also imported coal from Britain for iron-smelting in the Ruhr. France, far outdistanced by her great rival Germany as an industrial nation, was in a more vulnerable position because of her inferiority in the heavy industries which are war-potential. It was calculated that in 1914 the ratio of industrial potential was Germany 3, Great Britain 2, France 1.

Further complications were created in relations among the powers by the export not of men and goods, but of money. During the nineteenth century Britain had been the chief exporter of capital and London had been the monetary centre of the world. As in other respects her relative position had declined during the generation before 1914, and she had tended to transfer her investments from Europe to South America, the British Dominions, the United States, the Far East, and the tropics. This naturally shifted the direction and focus of her political and economic interests. In 1914 she had about £4,000 million invested overseas, in railways, docks, power works, mines, plantation companies, cables, and loans to foreign governments. This was roughly a quarter of her total wealth, and about half this overseas investment was in the lands of the

---

[1] In 1913 she produced 287.4 million tons, whilst the United States produced 508.9 million tons: Britain exported 76 million tons.

British Empire and Commonwealth. The French had the equivalent of £1,740 million in foreign investments, which was about a sixth of their national wealth: but only about one tenth of it was invested in the French colonies. Her heaviest investment was in Russia, to whom by 1914 the French had lent some £400 million. It was officially encouraged and was linked with the aims of foreign policy—to ensure a Russian alliance against Germany. German foreign investments were about £1,250 million, of which one fifth was in Africa, Asia, and the Ottoman Empire. The international economy rested on an international monetary system: this was sterling, based on the gold standard and managed by the City of London and the Bank of England.

. . . . .

The total effect of world economic developments was summarized like this by Professor J. H. Clapham:

The latest company age, which was in every sense international, completed the economic interlocking of the nations . . . Not merely were the nations buying from and selling to one another on a scale altogether unprecedented; not only was it possible for the United Kingdom to import four-fifths of her wheat, France a third of her coal, and Germany nearly all of her wool; but, owing to the easy transfer and movement of the joint-stock share, the nations had become each year part owners of one another's resources to an extraordinary degree. Companies with their main domicile in one country had manufacturing establishments, affiliated companies, "interests" of one kind or another, in a neighbouring country, or it might be in nearly all neighbouring and in many remote countries . . . With the railway and the telegraph the world had become one market. With the spread of a fairly uniform company law and of a uniform commercial practice, it was tending to become a single economic organism.[1]

But if the whole world had become, in this sense, one market, there were already signs that it would be a rapidly changing market, and that the European manufacturing nations might soon expect powerful new competitors in the market. Industrialism was fast spreading to Asia, where reservoirs of cheap labour could lower costs of production. This was the chief asset of Japan and of Russia. Japan's population in 1914 was more than 50 millions, and its average annual rate of increase was 1.2 per cent., so that by 1950 it was half as large again despite long periods of war. Korea, which she annexed in 1905, provided little outlet for emigration because it was already heavily populated. Japan was poor in all other natural resources desirable for an industrial power, for she had little coal or iron. The only raw material which she could hope to produce in abundance was silk, and the state provided capital to foster this industry. Under governmental encouragement western industrial methods were adopted, and huge industrial and commercial cities like Kobe, Osaka, Yokohama, and Nagasaki sprang up. At the turn of the century Japanese industrial production, like that of the United States, began to pass beyond the point of satisfying the home market and was seeking markets for exports overseas. Like Great Britain a century earlier, Japan soon became dependent upon her imports to feed herself and

[1] J. H. Clapham: *The Economic Development of France and Germany* 1815–1914, (1921), p. 401.

upon her exports to buy a large part of her raw materials. She aimed at becoming the workshop of the Far East, and at capturing for her textiles and other manufactures the markets of Asia and the Pacific. The preoccupations and difficulties of the other powers during the first world war were to give her tremendous opportunities for expansion. The sudden rise of Japan to the rank of a major world power in the Far East was perhaps the greatest single effect of the first world war.

Throughout the rest of Asia, and in Africa and South America, these tendencies were still much less fully developed. But they had begun. In Russia, India, and China industrialization, depending on power-driven machinery and transport, was beginning to have significant effects. In 1913 Russia was producing only half as much pig-iron as France, but nearly two-thirds as much steel. Her heavy industries and railways were being built, largely with the use of foreign capital. The completion of the Siberian railway led to a greater export of cotton goods to Chinese markets. But at the same time an industrial depression, especially in her heavy industries, set in and lasted until 1908. From 1910 until the outbreak of war her industrialization proceeded at a rate of progress comparable to that later planned by her Bolshevik governments. The coal mined in the Donetz basin doubled between 1905 and 1913, as did her total output of iron. Even so, nine Russians out of every ten still made their living from farming, and their methods of agriculture were extremely backward and primitive.

In India industrialization was connected with westernization, and that in turn with British rule. As

India was Britain's best customer the government of India had little incentive to promote industrialization, and until 1914 its policy was rather to permit Indian trade and industry to develop than to plan or promote it. India lacked the positive guiding hand of a paternalist government such as Tsarist Russia enjoyed, and this had the effect of exposing her economy to the competition of the much more highly industrialized British output. Her main industries remained, therefore, the plantation industries of tea, coffee, rubber, and tobacco and the textile industries of cotton and jute, with the heavy industries of coal, iron, and steel concentrated in Bengal and Bihar.

China, like India, had vast unexploited and even unexplored mineral resources, including iron ore, coal, tungsten, antimony, and tin. But her chief products were rice and cotton, and her industrialization had, by 1914, barely begun. Like the rest of Asia she remained basically a peasant country, with a low standard of subsistence because of lack of industrialization and because of backward and unscientific methods of agriculture.

In Africa the primary economic interest of the colonial powers was to find sources of cheap raw materials. Expansion in the growth of foodstuffs, which alone could raise the standard of living in the native populations, was a secondary concern: but in so far as concentration of capital and labour resources on the development of mining and of production of raw materials for export increased the flow of income within these territories, the standard of living was even improved. And provision of more stable order, and of improved communications and social services, probably conferred more social benefit on the native population than industrial development brought hardship.

In South America railways had been built (mainly with British capital and equipment) and again certain mineral resources had been developed. But the beginnings of a real industrial revolution in this great continent, as in parts of Asia, were to come only as a consequence of the first world war.

In 1914 the industrial powers of major importance were those of western Europe and the United States, with Japan already set for her immense development which revolutionized the balance of power in the Far East. But the other parts of the world, linked to the industrial powers either by subtle ties of political affiliation and alliance (like the Commonwealth and Russia) or by their role in the world economic system (like South America and the colonial territories), were bound to be vitally affected by a war between the major powers. War would dislocate international trade and the confidence on which the international monetary system and market rested. It would liquidate old debts and create new ones, and impoverish the rich to the advantage of those (like Japan) best able to seize the new opportunities. War, even more dramatically than progress in peace, would demonstrate the new interdependence of the continents.

§3. *Cultural Backcloth*

The Spanish philosopher, Ortega y Gasset, pointed out in a famous book the statistical fact on which the

culture of the twentieth century rests.[1] In the twelve
centuries before 1800, Europe reached a total population of 180 millions. Between 1800 and 1914 its population increased from 180 to 460 millions. The United
States was formed mainly from the overflow of Europe.
He argued that the dizzy rapidity of this increase meant
that 'heap after heap of human beings have been
dumped on to the historic scene at such a rate that it has
been difficult to saturate them with the traditional
culture . . . In the schools, which were such a source of
pride to the last century, it has been impossible to do
more than instruct the masses in the technique of
modern life; it has been found impossible to educate
them.' To this astounding fact, which must be kept in
mind in any study of world history since 1914, might
be added the comparable changes in Asia, as well as the
changes in Europe and America since 1914. Between
1815 and 1940 the population of India doubled from
nearly 200 to nearly 400 million. The population of
Java, under Dutch rule, increased from 5 million to
48 million in the same period. The population of Africa,
static or even declining previously, has in the same
period risen from 95 millions to 170 millions. That of
Latin America, similarly, has risen from 30 to 145
million. So not only has European culture been diluted
by the rapid growth of European masses and dispersed
more widely over the face of the earth, but the other
great continents have in consequence experienced the
same 'rise of the masses', with all that this entails in

---

[1] Ortega y Gasset: *The Revolt of the Masses* (*La Rebelión
de las Masas*), 1930.

cultural upheaval, in pressure on the world's resources of food and wealth, and in transformation of the whole of human geography.

Thinkers of many nationalities, besides Señor Ortega y Gasset, have sought the clue to an interpretation of twentieth-century history in some such principle: and they have served to emphasize different facets of this transformation of the world. In Germany, Spengler wrote of the cyclical development of civilizations and Haushofer of the changing geopolitical forces in the world. The Englishman Sir Halford Mackinder in 1919 interpreted European growth and power in terms of the great 'Heartland', which stretches from the Volga to Manchuria, and is the crucial area in a great 'World Island', including Europe, Asia, and Africa. A Frenchman, writing a few years later, described the 'two Europes' which had arisen since 1870: the 'inner zone' or the 'Europe of steam', bounded by an imaginary line joining Glasgow, Stockholm, Danzig, Trieste, Florence, and Barcelona, wherein heavy industry and rapid transport, scientific laboratories and the urge for greater constitutional liberties were located; and the 'outer zone', including Ireland, most of Iberia and Italy, and all Europe east of Germany and Czechoslovakia, predominantly agricultural and peasant, and thus depending upon the inner zone for its borrowed inventions and capital, its economic progress, and its culture. Beyond this outer zone lay the vast areas of Asia and Africa, still more 'backward' in technical development and still more dependent on the inner zone for their prosperity. All such historical and geographical interpretations of recent world history throw some light on the facts, and it is unnecessary to accept any one of them as containing the whole truth. But in conjunction they emphasize the central themes of recent world history.[1]

These are, first, the explosive impact of European migration, trade, technical invention, and production on the rest of the world. Such an impact carries with it great repercussions on the culture of all areas. Secondly, there is the transformation of human life in industrialized society itself. The characteristics of this transformation have normally been the rapid growth of urban centres and factory production, carrying with them all the familiar British nineteenth-century problems of human adjustment to a more cramped physical environment and mechanical working discipline. This has been accompanied by a raising of the level of literacy, popular education, a popular press, and other media of shaping mass opinion, and the development of new social organizations of great complexity which demand the services of skilled technicians, managers and administrators. Thirdly, such developments have been accompanied by an intensification of nationalist feelings and prejudices, by new conflicts of organized economic and social interests such as employers' associations, trade unions, and professional groups, and by efforts to harmonize these conflicts within the national com-

---

[1] Amongst others may be mentioned Arnold J. Toynbee's *A Study of History* (1934–54), P. A. Sorokin's *Social and Cultural Dynamics* (1937–41), and Alfred A. Kroeber's *Configurations of Culture Growth* (1944).

munity by means of the democratic machinery of representative government and universal suffrage. This pattern of development, beginning in nineteenth-century Britain and spreading quickly to western Europe and to the United States, has in the twentieth century spread in some measure to every continent and country. By 1914 there were only indications that this was likely to happen. The process had not, except in Japan, gone far enough to reveal its probable consequences and complexities.

The full possibilities of rapid communication and transport had not become apparent whilst aviation and radio had not developed, and the motor car was in its infancy. The social implications of mass-production and extreme specialization of labour were still in the future.[1] The media of mass opinion and entertainment had evolved as far as the popular and often sensational press, which played a large part in moulding the nationalist rivalries and anxieties of the decade before 1914. The cinema existed, but on a small scale. Broadcasting and the vast sports stadia made possible by electrical amplification were delights still unknown. In literate countries the detective story and the pulp magazine were ousting the more serious novel and the Bible as the general literary diet: though gutter

[1] But it was on 6 January 1914 that Henry Ford dramatically announced that in place of the previous minimum wage-rate of $2.34 for a nine-hour day he would pay a minimum of $5 for an eight-hour day. He rightly calculated that not only would men do better work in shorter hours, but that much of the extra they earned would in future be spent on motor-cars. This was a landmark in the history of United States labour.

publications, as always, made their appearance. In most
western European countries (apart from Spain and
Portugal) elementary education on a national scale had
existed for a generation, but the tone of art, music, and
literature was set more by the *élites* than by the tastes
of the masses. Education, still something to be prized
and often paid for, was assumed to require effort and
some sacrifice on the part of the recipient. France,
Switzerland, and since 1910 Portugal, were the only
republics in Europe. Crowned heads and titled aristocrats
attracted the attention and interest which were soon to
be shared with footballers, film-stars, and radio perform-
ers. The age of mass entertainment was just beginning.

Philosophy and science were much concerned with
studying the phenomena of the new age. Darwinism
was still a matter for violent controversy, and acceptance of its principles a sign of progressive enlighten-
ment. Psychology and sociology, with the work of Sig-
mund Freud, Gabriel Tarde, and Émile Durkheim,
were finding a new scientific basis and new avenues of
progress. Henri Bergson was seeking a philosophical
explanation of the more mysterious forces of human
life and activity, whilst economists explored the equally
mysterious phenomena of mass unemployment and
distress.[1] All serious students of the problems of man
in society were aware of the novelties of their changing
society and of some of the dangers in the changes. The

[1] William Beveridge's *Unemployment* appeared in 1909, and
Bergson's main works had been translated into English before
1914.

most impressive advances were being made in the medical and biological sciences, and in the physical and technological sciences. The great cleavage in philosophy was between those who held that a similarly whole-hearted application of scientific methods to the study of man and society would yield equally satisfactory results, and those who doubted or denied this. This cleavage, which can be traced throughout the contrasts between rival schools of literature and art as well as philosophy, has been perhaps the main feature of world culture in the twentieth century.

From the nineteenth century was inherited the powerful tradition of positivism, associated with the name of Auguste Comte who elaborated and systematized it. It had by 1914 become the orthodox creed of many influential philosophers. Its basic belief was that the philosopher should adopt the scientist's criterion of truth: a theory or principle is true in so far as it enables men to foresee, and in some measure control, the physical universe. From this it was tempting to move on to pragmatism, summarized by the American philosopher, William James, as meaning 'We cannot reject any hypothesis if consequences useful to life flow from it'. This mental outlook was in some ways the heir of utilitarianism, and chimed so conveniently with an age of industrialism and material progress that it won wide acceptance. Its counterpart was 'realism' and 'naturalism' in art: which found expression in the novels of social significance, the drama of Ibsen, Shaw and Galsworthy, and strongly intellectualist tendencies in all the arts.

In strong reaction against this outlook were philosophical arguments ranging from the amoralism and anti-intellectualism of the German Friedrich Nietzsche (who died in 1900) to the exaltation of intuition as against intellect in the writings of Henri Bergson (who died in 1941). Although they had some affinities with the early nineteenth-century romantic movement, these ideas tended to be aristocratic and anti-democratic. In art they had their counterpart in the novels of Marcel Proust (most of whose work appeared after 1918), in the revival of symbolism, and in the cubism of Matisse and Picasso. In some countries a powerful rearguard action was also fought by the idealist philosophers, led by the Oxford Hegelians in England and by Gentile and Croce in Italy.

But the unorthodox philosophers and artists were ahead of both political theory and general opinion in their challenge. The discovery that men—especially men in the mass—were prompted in their actions at least as much by irrational impulses and instincts as by rational or intellectual considerations had not yet thrown into disarray the assumptions of the older radicalism and liberalism. In Britain the Fabians regarded themselves as students and practitioners of 'social engineering': and if there was already much talk of the role of violence and of the social 'myth' in the forces which mould modern industrial and urban society, that was still associated with wild syndicalists like Sorel (whose *Reflections on Violence*, much influenced by Nietzsche and Bergson, appeared in 1906). It was not taken too seriously by most liberal thinkers or practical men, just as cubism was treated as freakish. Even the conjunction in Britain of movements of extreme violence such as the big strikes, the suffragette agitation, and the Irish troubles was regarded as a temporary disorder which firm handling by the government could adequately quell. Revolutions were, by now, things that happened only in eastern Europe or in Latin America. Had not even France contrived to keep the Third Republic for forty years?

The gulf between political thinking and reality had its counterpart in a growing divorce of the artist from society. The creative artist suffered from the growth of specialization, and was regarded as a special kind of specialist, likely to be incomprehensible to the general public. Novelists and dramatists concerned with the social ills of their time—a Tolstoy and a Wells, an Ibsen and a Shaw—remained generally comprehensible because they were in the naturalistic tradition. But painting, poetry, and music suffered from an indifference and lack of sympathy in their public. (The cult of Charles Péguy came only after his death in battle in 1914.) The result was obscurity and technicality on the part of the creative artists, and a corresponding impoverishment of public taste. The artist was tempted to indulge either in capricious self-expression, such as cubism and extreme impressionism, or to seek escape, like Gauguin, in exotic parts of the world still free from industrialism.

Yet the new incoherency—which after the war was to breed 'surrealism'—had certain common roots with positivism and science. The urge towards materialism, ever present in the nineteenth century, had found increasingly crude and over-simplified expressions. Darwinism gave place to the 'social Darwinists', who saw human progress as a product of physical struggle, and even to the racialists, such as Houston Stewart Chamberlain, who saw in blood the clue to human history. A decline in religious faith and observance was perhaps more a symptom than a cause of this materialism, for nineteenth-century religion had often been compatible with a heavy materialism of outlook. Perhaps it had always been present in the very devotion to scientific progress which nineteenth-century events had encouraged. It seemed self-evident that only by studying the material world and how it works, and only by doing so with the experimental techniques of science, could knowledge be accumulated and real progress made. But if the new science of psychology revealed hitherto unknown aspects of human nature, was it not equally 'realistic' to explore and emphasize these, in the process attacking not only the prevailing intellectualism but even the rationalist assumptions on which science itself had developed? The result, by 1914, was confusion of minds and a certain bewilderment.

.   .   .   .   .

The world scene in 1914, in its broadest terms, was one of more intense economic interdependence combined with more severe political separateness; of social and economic progress, in the sense of higher standards of living and comfort, combined with growing tensions within society between capital and labour; of great material progress combined with cultural impoverishment and confusion. It was clearly a world in a state of flux and of rapid transformation. Yet in most western countries, as compared with the world of 1950, it was a time of security and optimism. The steps by which that world became the world of 1950 is the theme of the remaining chapters of this book.

Chapter Two

THE FIRST WORLD WAR, 1914–1918

§1. *Issues Involved*

THERE are many ways in which the war of 1914–1918 was unprecedented and, in human history, entirely novel. Previous wars, such as the French Revolutionary and Napoleonic wars, had lasted longer and had involved as many peoples. But this was the first war of the masses, which as already shown had increased so vastly in size since 1815. It was the first general conflict between the highly organized nation-states of the twentieth century, able to command the energies of all their citizens or subjects, to mobilize the productive capacity of heavy industries, and to utilize all the resources of modern technology to find new methods of destruction. It was also the first war on a scale large enough to dislocate the economy of the world which, during the previous century, had become so closely knit. It was probable from the first that such a war would prove to be not only more destructive of human life and material wealth than any previous wars, but also more far-reaching, incalculable, and uncontrollable in its aftermath. It is the first major war in history in which there was so much disparity between its consequences and achievements and the avowed intentions and purposes of those who first went to war. For this reason it is necessary to keep sharply distinct the issues which were avowedly involved when it began, and the issues which came to be involved in it before it ended: and equally distinct from both, the consequences which we now know to have flowed from it.

When the Empire of Austria-Hungary went to war with Serbia in 1914 and when Russia mobilized on Serbia's side, the nineteenth-century Eastern Question reached its culmination. The multi-national dynastic empire of Austria-Hungary could not tolerate the growth of Serbia without incurring the risk that she would still further disintegrate into her national components. The dynastic Empire of Tsarist Russia could not tolerate Austrian expansion into the Balkans without losing her own appeal to the Slav peoples of eastern Europe. When Germany mobilized on the side of Austria-Hungary and France on the side of Russia and Serbia, it was because neither could afford to lose the support of its ally in its security calculations against the other. When Germany invaded Belgium, whose neutrality she and other western powers had undertaken to respect, it was because the Schlieffen Plan, drawn up several years earlier against just such a contingency, made it imperative for the German armies to attempt a knock-out blow at northern France and at Paris before Russia could strike and before possible British support could become effective. When Great Britain declared war on Germany, it was partly because Germany had thus violated a joint undertaking to respect Belgian neutrality, and partly because both the naval agreements made with France and the fear of German naval power made it necessary for Britain to stand by France in face of this attack. When Japan declared war on

Germany it was to seize her concessions in China and her
islands in the Pacific. When, after some delay, the Ottoman Turkish Empire and Bulgaria joined Germany, it
was because one was the enemy of Russia and the other
nursed grievances against Serbia. When, in 1915, Italy
joined Britain, France, and Russia it was because, in the
secret Treaty of London of that year, she was promised
territorial gains at the expense of Turkey and Austria,
and led to expect colonial gains.

Thus the entry of each of the belligerents was determined by considerations of national security and
national power. If, as the optimistic Cobdenites of the
nineteenth century believed, trade was a bond of interest and friendship between nations, Germany and
Britain should not have found themselves on opposing
sides, and Germany should have been on excellent
terms with most of her European neighbours. As Lord
Keynes pointed out, 'We sent more exports to Germany than to any other country in the world except
India, and we bought more from her than from any
other country in the world except the United States'.[1]
She was the best customer of Russia, Austria-Hungary,
Italy, Switzerland, Belgium, Holland, and Norway: and
the third best customer of France. Every country to the
east of her did more than a quarter of its whole trade
with her. These commercial links, which had all developed so extensively after 1890, did nothing to prevent or to alter the alignment of the belligerents. They
served only to aggravate the economic dislocation

[1] J. M. Keynes: *The Economic Consequences of the Peace*
(1919), p. 15.

caused by Germany's defeat in 1918. The issues had
very much to do with mutual fears and distrusts on the
continent of Europe, but very little to do with colonial
rivalries outside it. Although colonial territories were
drawn upon for levies of troops, and the overseas
Dominions rallied to the side of Britain, the war was in
essence a European war fought about European issues.
For that reason its original label of 'the Great War' was
more apt than its subsequent label of 'First world war'.
If it could have been ended, as the Germans hoped and
planned, by 1915, with the decisive defeat of France
and the financial and administrative collapse of Russia,
and without the participation of Great Britain, it would
have resulted in the consolidation of the dynastic continental empires of central and eastern Europe. Its chief
consequence would have been a vast extension of
German power into the Balkans and the eastern marchlands, with doors opened to the Near and Far East and
to overseas colonial expansion. In that event it would
be accounted historically not the first world war, but
the fourth of the imperial German wars;[1] and it would
almost certainly have led to a fifth which might, indeed,
have been a world war. In this sense, it was above all
the participation of the British Commonwealth, the
most world-wide of all the powers, which turned it into a
world war. The British refusal to remain neutral as Germany had hoped also meant that the United States would
eventually have to abandon its policy of neutrality:

[1] The first three being Bismarck's wars of 1864 against
Denmark, of 1866 against Austria-Hungary, and of 1870
against France.

for the participation of the Commonwealth ensured that it would be a long war, in which America was unlikely to permit the protective screen of the British navy to be too much weakened without herself joining in to assure her own security.

But although, with all the advantages of historical hindsight, we can now see these implications to have been present from the moment in 1914 when the Schlieffen Plan failed, they were not apparent at the time. Once war had begun the motives for continuing it changed. France had to go on fighting for sheer survival, and because she was invaded: so had Russia and Serbia. Germany, faced with the traditional horror of war on two fronts, had to strike desperately first in the west and then in the east, to preserve herself from invasion and collapse. The Austrian and Turkish Empires had only the alternatives of war or internal collapse. Great Britain alone had a measure of choice, though she could not risk an ultimate German victory, in the sense that she could plan for a long war of blockade and attrition without any immediate risk of being invaded. The United States, by the same token, had a wider margin of choice and of time in which to make it.

Until 1917 the alignment of the powers permitted of no clear ideological issues. The parliamentary and democratic states, Britain, France, and Belgium, were allied with the most reactionary of all the dynastic Empires, Tsarist Russia. Germany was allied with her former opponent and rival, Austria-Hungary, and her potential victim, the Ottoman Empire. The western powers claimed to be fighting German militarism and imperialism, but they were themselves colonial imperial powers and France was traditionally one of the most militarist nations in Europe. Idealistic claims were valid only so far as the western powers were in fact supporting the cause of national self-determination for Serbia and the important cause of the sanctity of treaty obligations in the case of Belgium. Otherwise such claims cloaked the realities of bitter international fears and jealousies which were the heritage of the years since 1870.

But from 1917 it was possible to speak with validity of a clash of ideologies. When Russia, in the throes of internal revolution, signed the Treaty of Brest-Litovsk and withdrew from the war, and when the United States entered on the side of the western Allies, the alignment became clear. Henceforth it was, in the main, a war between the western maritime powers which were also colonial powers and democratic in outlook, and the central and eastern dynastic powers which were continental empires and were hostile to the ideals of democracy. This transformation of the whole nature of the war which took place in its third year not only predetermined its result, since American weight ensured a western victory, but also set the stage for that apparent triumph of the ideals and institutions of democratic government which dominated the decade of the nineteen-twenties. This outcome, it must be repeated, was in the minds of none of the original participants in 1914. In this way the greatest of the nineteenth-century wars of nationalism turned dramatically into the first of the twentieth-century wars of ideology.

The war lasted fifty-two months, which by comparison with Bismarckian *Blitzkriegs* was long, but by comparison with other general European wars was short. What was new was not the duration but the ferocious and concentrated intensity of it: the speed with which great industrial powers proved that they could mobilize new armies and supplies, transport them hundreds of miles, and hurl them against one another in bitter self-destruction. The two sides showed themselves so nearly equal in their skill and ability to do this that the chief feature of the war in the west was prolonged deadlock, with so much concentrated power on each side that it seemed the irresistible force had met the immovable obstacle. Thus, paradoxically, the war of speed and rapid movement became on the field of battle a war of stalemate and attrition.

This peculiarly exhausting nature of modern warfare had importance for the very nature of the issues involved. Each government was driven to squeeze its people harder and harder for further effort, not only in its armed forces but also on the civilian front and in industrial production. Britain did not introduce conscription until 1916 and France did not introduce income-tax to finance the war until 1917: but both had to resort to these essentials of total war in the end. The naval blockade of Germany and the U-Boat sinkings of Britain's vital imports of food opened up hostilities on the home fronts. The war became increasingly like a Darwinian struggle for survival. The appeals for ever more concerted and strenuous national efforts not only intensified nationalist sentiments: they were accom-

panied by more and more promises of fuller social justice after the war—of 'making the world safe for democracy', of 'homes fit for heroes', of full recognition for
the rights of 'national self-determination', and the rest.
In this way the very character of warfare helped to in-
fuse more idealism into the peace-aims of the Allies,
and encouraged greater expectations of freedom and
equality in peace. The argument was increasingly heard
that if human organization and resolve could achieve
such marvels for war, a comparable effort in peace
could remove all social ills. Thus the war greatly extended the nineteenth-century list of social evils regarded as remediable by human effort, and not to be
tolerated as inherent in a malignant providence. It
encouraged a faith in perfectionism, a readiness to
experiment in social overhaul and economic planning,
which the Bolshevik Revolution was in time to strengthen even more. The welfare state was much promoted
by the warfare state.

The defeat and withdrawal of Russia demonstrated
that absolutist states were ill fitted to survive the strains
of such warfare, and the moral was soon underlined by
the similar collapse of Austria-Hungary and the Ottoman Empire. At the same time the entry of the United
States infused a new and even more optimistic idealism
into the peace-aims of the Allies. President Wilson
made himself peculiarly the spokesman of idealism and
perfectionism. His famous Fourteen Points of January
1918 have been much misunderstood by those who have
discussed them without reading them. Far from being
general statements of vague moral principles, they

include a list of quite specific purposes which the Allies had already proclaimed they would pursue in the settlement after the war: such purposes as the restoration of Alsace and Lorraine to France, the liberation of Belgium, the reconstitution of Poland, and the German evacuation of Russian and Balkan lands. But mixed with these indisputably just and attainable aims was a series of more debatable Wilsonian propositions: 'open covenants openly arrived at', which meant an end not only to secret treaties but to discreet diplomacy; 'freedom of the seas alike in peace and in war'; removal of barriers and inequalities in international trade; the reduction of armaments; readjustments of colonial claims and possessions; a redrawing of the map of Europe, especially of eastern Europe, along lines of 'national self-determination'; and above all the creation of a new international organization to prevent war. Such ideas were elaborated by the President in a series of speeches and pronouncements,[1] and acquired a strong appeal as an enlightened liberal programme for a new kind of peacemaking. This powerful formulation of moral peace-aims chimed with the more realistic contrast between the Allied Powers and their enemies. Just as it was the cynical German violation of Belgian rights which brought Britain unitedly into the war, so the United States were brought in by the inhuman pro-

[1] Especially the 'Four Principles' (February), the 'Four Ends' (July) and the 'Five Particulars' (September). These later pronouncements were increasingly idealistic and general in tone, and even included 'the destruction of every arbitrary power anywhere . . .' and 'no leagues or alliances or special covenants and understandings within the general and common family of the League of Nations'.

clamation of unrestricted submarine warfare. The Allies were able to appeal directly, as a part of their psychological warfare, to the divided and repressed nationalities of eastern Europe, because their success would automatically disrupt the dynastic empires: and this appeal could be made all the more strongly after the defeat of Russia, whose alliance had in this respect embarrassed the Allies. Several factors in this way conspired to make the war for the Allies, by 1917–1918, a moral crusade for the characteristic liberal ideals of respect for international obligations, national independence and self-determination, and the values of democracy.

Yet this powerful idealism was, so to speak, superimposed upon the older more separatist national purposes, and did not replace them. The Allies were by no means willing to endorse all Wilson's propositions. France, being the main western battlefield, insisted that Germany should make some reparation for war damage. Britain was doubtful about the notion of freedom of the seas 'in peace and war', which would have made her blockade of Germany impossible. Both were hesitant about erecting national self-determination into what Wilson was apt to describe as 'an imperative principle of action', and foresaw the difficulties of attempting to apply it logically to the tangle of nationalities in the Balkans. The French tested any settlement not by its conformity to abstract justice so much as by how far it fulfilled the basic ends for which France had fought: her survival as a nation-state and her own security against a recurrence of German invasion.

Britain judged it by the extent to which it removed permanently the menace of German naval rivalry and restored a more equable balance of power in Europe. Italy judged it by the degree to which it fulfilled the ends she had stipulated in the Treaty of London, and by this standard she was from the first a dissatisfied power. The Balkan nationalities judged it by how far it enabled them to fulfil their national aspirations for unity and independence, and here too it was inevitable that some should be disappointed, since their aims were often in conflict. Thus, although the war as it proceeded moved from a phase of nationalistic struggle to one of moral and liberal idealism, it ended as a mixture of the two: and the main characteristic of the problems confronting the peacemakers in 1919 was precisely this perplexing blend of realistic and moral claims.

§2. *Service of Mars*

Assessment of the place of the war in modern world history requires some reckoning of the human effort and sacrifice involved. Warfare was much less mechanized than it had become by the second world war, so it was primarily a war of soldiers, of infantry and artillery. Even motor transport was still a novelty. Despite the use of naval blockade by each side, naval combat between capital units was slight after the Battle of Jutland in 1916, so it was a war more of soldiers than of sailors. Aviation was used for reconnaissance, artillery observation, and occasional bombing: but bombing of rear areas took place only during the last few months. Although the efforts of the home front in production and civilian morale were throughout of considerable importance, and much more important than in former wars, it was still a war more of soldiers than of civilians. Until the spread of starvation in Russia and Germany and the great influenza epidemic at the end of the war, it was soldiers and not civilians who were wounded or killed. German Zeppelin raids on London did little damage. Given the long war of attrition in the west and the massive troop-clashes of the eastern front, the crucial problem for both sides throughout was the enlistment, training, transport, and equipment of millions of men in uniform. It was the efforts of governments to grapple with this problem which drove the effects of the war deep into the heart of practically every family within each nation. With the exception of the United States, which at the armistice had 4 million men under arms but which had entered in time enough to be decisive and yet also late enough to incur only 115,000 deaths,[1] the service of Mars in Europe meant the systematic massacre of 10 millions of men, and mainly of men under 40 years of age.

Until the very last phases of the war advantage lay heavily on the side of the defence, although leading military theory in both Germany and France favoured a strategy of the offensive. The main reason for the war of attrition was the machine-gun. Against it infantry

---

[1] Of these, less than half were killed in actual battle. The rest died mainly from disease, including some 25,000 soldiers who died in the great influenza epidemic. The United Kingdom lost 744,000 and the rest of the Commonwealth some 202,000. France and her colonies lost nearly 1,400,000, Germany 1,855,000, Austria-Hungary nearly 1,500,000.

armed with rifles, bayonets, and grenades could advance only after long and costly preparations of heavy artillery fire. Each side therefore dug into trenches defended with barbed-wire entanglements and machine-guns, and could be dislodged only after long preparations and at heavy cost in lives. In April 1915 at Ypres the Germans used poison-gas as an auxiliary to artillery fire in preparation for attack. It proved indecisive, but each side thereafter used gas until the end of the war. The Battle of the Somme in the summer of 1916 illustrates the problem. The Allies mustered 2,000 heavy cannon behind a ten-mile front, and continuously for a week they bombarded the enemy trenches. In the first day's attack the British lost 60,000 men. After a month they had advanced only two and a half miles. In the whole battle the Germans lost 500,000 men, the British and French 600,000. Each advance would find the enemy entrenched a mile or two further back, and the whole process of preparatory shelling would have to begin again. Major offensives thus took a long time to prepare and usually achieved very little territorial gain. But to hold such lines of defence, and even more to mount so costly an attack, needed millions of men. The use of whole armies, massed as battering-rams, was the most ingenious form of warfare which the art of generalship on either side could devise. It seldom resulted in breaking the line of defence, and at best pressed it a few miles further back.

Only two weapons could wrest the advantage away from the defence. One was the tank and motorized column. The British invented the tank and used it

tentatively in the battle of the Somme. But the military
mind was slow to perceive its possibilities, and its role
was not decisive. The other was the use of aviation for
bombing, which was adopted only in the final phase of
the war. Meanwhile, perhaps none of the great battles
of the western front, between the first Battle of the
Marne in September 1914 which frustrated the
Schlieffen Plan, and the last Battle of the Marne in the
summer of 1918 which achieved a break-through, could
be called really decisive. Most were unprofitable because the advances and gains made were out of all proportion to the costs. In 1916 the French held the German attack at Verdun at a cost of about one-third of a
million men each. In 1917 the British in the Battle of
Passchendaele advanced five miles near Ypres at a cost
of 400,000 men. Until 1918 the only gains of any major
battle in the west were the negative yet important ones
of simply frustrating and holding the enemy. Hence the
irony and the paradox that the so-called stalemate and
war of attrition in the west consumed men as cannon-
fodder at a rate vastly greater than any previous war in
history. The French calculated that, between August
1914 and February 1917, one Frenchman was killed
every minute.

Nor was the war of greater movement on the eastern
front any less costly in human life, although the reasons
there were somewhat different. Not only was the front
too long to be held by defence-trenches, but the Russians lacked machine-guns and artillery. The Germans,
with superior weapons and organization, could therefore make dramatic advances. But Russia's greatest

assets were space and a vast resource of manpower, and
she could afford to squander both more lavishly without
suffering defeat. In 1915 alone she lost two million men
killed, wounded, or taken prisoner, and the Germans
were far within Lithuania and White Russia. In 1916
she lost another million. But the Russian armies still
held the field and refused to make an armistice. The
absorption of whole German armies in the east, despite
German skill in rapid transportation of men and supplies from one front to the other, was inevitably a great
asset to the western Allies. Their aim was naturally to
keep Russia in the war at all costs, and to do this they
showed readiness to promise her gains at Turkey's expense after the war, as well as to help finance her war-
effort in every way possible. In this policy they succeeded to a remarkable degree. In 1917, when the Tsar
was overthrown and a new Provisional Government set
up, that Government kept Russia in the war. It was
only after the Bolshevik Revolution that Trotsky was
sent to negotiate peace with Germany which was signed
at Brest-Litovsk on 3 March 1918. The nationalities
within the western Russian borders had already, with
German encouragement, asserted their claim to independence: and by the Treaty the Bolsheviks agreed to
the loss of Finland, Russian Poland, the Ukraine, and
the three Baltic areas of Lithuania, Latvia, and Estonia.
Although Germany still had to maintain some forces in
the east to enforce the Treaty she was now freed from
the war on two fronts and could move whole armies to
the western front. She also gained additional supplies
from the Ukraine which helped her to survive the

lockade. But these gains came too late to offset American reinforcements on the other side.

They were offset, too, by the collapse of all Germany's major allies. As late as 1917 both Turkey and Austria-Hungary were holding firm and even gaining victories. The Turks, reinforced by German officers, had successfully held the Dardanelles against British and French military and naval attack in 1915. In 1916 Serbia and Rumania (which had recently and inopportunely entered the war) were overrun by Germany and Austria-Hungary, and in 1917 the Italians were routed at Caporetto. But within both empires the Allies had been able to mobilize insurgent nationalities, and internal tensions were severe. They were ready to split apart as soon as defeat seemed imminent, and gave Germany constant anxieties. For these reasons, when the end came it came swiftly and catastrophically. Just as no power had plans ready for a long war in 1914, so now in 1918 none expected it to end so suddenly. Peace in 1918 caught statesmen even more unprepared than war had caught them in 1914.

War in the west ended, as it had begun, with a momentous decision of the German High Command. In each year of the war they had devised a new plan aimed at bringing the war to a quick and decisive end. The Schlieffen Plan, as executed by Moltke in 1914, had aimed at enveloping northern France and Paris in one knock-out blow. It had failed because he had been compelled to remove forces to the east and weaken the power of the blow, and because the British Expeditionary Force and the French had checked it. The efforts of

F

Hindenburg, in 1915, to knock out Russia met with
similar frustration. The attack on Verdun, designed to
'bleed France to death', had been held by Pétain. The
submarine campaign of 1917 had nearly succeeded at
first, but had been foiled by effective anti-submarine
measures and by American aid. The Ludendorff Plan
of 1918, to force a wedge between the British and
French forces, was defeated by the unified command of
Foch and by the arrival of powerful British and American reinforcements and supplies. Now, in the autumn
of 1918, with Germany strained to the utmost, her
allies surrendering, and American troops landing in
Europe at a rate of 250,000 every month, the German
High Command notified its government that it could
not win the war and recommended that Germany
should sue for an armistice. General Ludendorff
pressed that a special democratic government should
be formed for the purpose, accompanied by such constitutional reforms as would ensure that the responsibility for accepting the terms of defeat should not rest
on the shoulders of the Army and the aristocracy which
had brought about defeat. Meanwhile President
Wilson, for quite contrary reasons, was insisting that
peace should be made only with a more democratic
Germany. Prince Max of Baden, a liberal, headed a
coalition which included the socialists. Faced with a
mutiny at Kiel on 3 November and a general strike on
9 November, Kaiser Wilhelm II abdicated. Germany
was proclaimed a republic, and two days later—on
11 November—an armistice was signed. The High
Command had snatched victory for itself from nationa

defeat. The war ended with German armies in France but no enemy forces on German soil, so that the myth that the Army had been undefeated could be created. And it remained for the new democratic republic to shoulder the blame for signing the armistice and accepting the terms of the peace. The military caste which had made Prussia the core of the German Reich lived to fight another day. Even the Kaiser, soon to be condemned as a war criminal, lived on peacefully in neutral Holland until 1942. Such was the German revolution of 1918, from which the parliamentary Weimar Republic was born.

Meanwhile, before the promised peace conference could meet in Paris, many other nations had taken charge of their own destiny. In October 1918 the Allies had given recognition to the various national committees representing the national groups of the Austro-Hungarian Empire. On 13 November the last of the Habsburg Emperors went into exile. Austria and Hungary each became a republic. New states of Czechoslovakia under Czech leadership, Yugoslavia under Serbian leadership, a resuscitated Poland, and an enlarged Rumania appeared on the map. Their governments and frontiers remained undefined in detail, but their claim to be constituted and recognized as new national states was now irresistible. In the Near East a group of Arab States similarly emerged from the debris of the Turkish Empire. Fighting continued in Turkey long after the German armistice, because the Greeks invaded Anatolia with British and French backing. Turkish resistance was rallied by Mustapha Kemal who by 1923, with some aid from the new Soviet Government of Russia, expelled the Greeks and the Allies from the Anatolian peninsula. A new Turkish Republic, under the strong rule of Kemal, was proclaimed in 1923. From the eastern shores of the Baltic down to the Persian gulf a vast belt of new states was created. The old empires had exploded into splinters, leaving between Europe and Asia a restless area of new nationalities, still nursing grievances against one another and looking for support to one or another of the great powers. In the longer perspective of history this was perhaps the most momentous single change in Europe produced by the war.

It had been made possible by the remarkable fact that both Russia and Germany had been defeated, so that there existed along the eastern marchlands what has been called a 'power-vacuum'. The fate of intermediate states such as Poland, situated between two powerful neighbours such as Germany and Russia, has normally been dependent on their making terms with one or other of their stronger neighbours. With both pressures simultaneously removed, such states were able to assert their complete independence of either, though looking inevitably to the western powers, particularly France, as a source of external support. France, anxious to find allies in the east both as a bulwark against the western spread of Bolshevism and as a weapon against German resurgence, was willing enough to play the role of sponsor to these new states. To this extent she was willing to back Woodrow Wilson's principle of national self-determination as applied in eastern Europe. In this way a territorial settlement of frontiers and a diplomatic system of alliances emerged, both resting on the assumption that this power-vacuum in the east could be preserved, or at least could be adequately filled by the new states. Any recovery of military and economic power by either Germany or Russia would be bound to challenge this arrangement. In the event both powers regained their might by 1936: and there followed inevitably a series of European crises which resulted in a second world war when Germany and Russia allied together to re-partition Poland. In this and other ways, the seeds of the second world war were present in the culmination of the first.

The shift of power in the Pacific by 1918 was to prove almost equally momentous. Japan, as already mentioned, within the first year of war seized upon German concessions in China and upon German Pacific Islands —the Marshalls and the Carolines. In 1915 she forced upon China most of her Twenty-One Demands, which gave her a large measure of control over northern China and South Manchuria. She prospered by capturing former European markets in Asia and in South America, and carried much of the trade of Asia in her ships. In the Pacific, too, with a weak China, a defeated Russia, and the United States and British Commonwealth pre-occupied, there was a temporary vacuum of power which the Japanese were best equipped and most ambitious to fill. The agreements reached at the Washington Conference of 1921 postponed the conflict for ten years, by fixing naval parity between the Commonwealth and the United States, and the strength of Japan in capital ships at 60 per cent. of the British and

American figures. For a time, the pre-war balance of power in the Pacific seemed to have been restored. But here, too, the legacy of the war which the peacemakers could do little to change contained the conditions of future conflict. The service of Mars had been undertaken on long-term indentures.

§3. *Post-War Settlement*

Representatives of 'the allied or associated belligerent powers' met at Paris in January 1919 to lay down the conditions of peace. They included spokesmen not only of the main Allies and succession states, but also of those powers which had, in the later phases, broken off diplomatic relations with the enemy powers. These were Bolivia, Ecuador, Peru, and Uruguay. China and Siam, having at the last moment declared war, were included amongst the allied belligerents. Former enemy states were excluded, so all the treaties except that of Lausanne with Turkey in 1923 were dictated and not negotiated.

The conduct and the main lines of the settlement were determined by the 'Big Three'—President Wilson of the United States, Georges Clemenceau of France, and David Lloyd George the Prime Minister of Britain. Japan and Italy were at first included in the inner circle of leading powers, but soon absented themselves. Wilson's chief aims were to ensure the application of the general principles he had enunciated as necessary for a just peace, and to set up the League of Nations. In order to get general agreement to the League he was driven to compromise on the application of his general principles in the territorial settlement, and consoled himself with the reflection that parts of the territorial and political settlement which he disliked could in time be improved, at more leisure, through the working of the League as an agency of conciliation and peaceful change. The actual settlement was, in consequence, a series of bargains and compromises between the high-minded but often unrealistic desires of Wilson, the nationalistic and intensely realistic demands of Clemenceau, and the somewhat unstable and oppor-tunistic aims of Lloyd George.

The settlement, and particularly that part of it in-cluded in the Treaty of Versailles made with Germany, has often been criticized for being such a patchwork of conflicting purposes. Yet it was not necessarily the worse for that. What else was so large an international conference for, if it was not to find the highest common measure of agreement amongst states whose aims and interests in many ways conflicted? Wilson's general principles, had they been applied consistently, would have had disastrous and often absurd results: yet his enormous personal prestige and his persistence did succeed in infusing some wider and more lasting vision into the arrangements. The exaggerated demands of Clemenceau and Lloyd George, had they not been moderated, would have resulted in a Carthaginian peace: yet they did serve to remind Wilson of the grim-mer realities of European politics. A more serious critic-ism is that the settlement was not only a patchwork, but that it was harsh in the wrong places and lenient in the wrong ways. How far this criticism is valid may best be judged from the main arrangements made and from the degree of permanence they proved to have.

Belgian independence was restored, and the provinces of Alsace and Lorraine were returned to France, from whom Germany had taken them in 1871. This was indisputably just. France also gained ownership of the Saar coalfields, and the area was to be administered for fifteen years by a League of Nations Commission. In 1935, after the prescribed plebiscite among the population, it was returned to Germany. This arrangement, again, worked reasonably well. The Rhineland was to remain in allied military occupation for fifteen years, as a guarantee that Germany would fulfil the Treaty. This was a compromise, and from the French viewpoint a most unsatisfactory one. Clemenceau, urged by Foch, had at first demanded indefinite control of the Rhine bridgeheads as a military guarantee of French security. The United States and Britain refused to agree, and persuaded the French to accept instead a joint Anglo-American guarantee to support France immediately if she were again attacked by Germany. But when the Treaty was not ratified by the American Senate this guarantee lapsed on the United States' side, and Britain then claimed that this invalidated her part of the bargain. France, in consequence, felt that she had been tricked into surrendering her material security for what now proved to be a worthless diplomatic assurance. Hence her feverish quest for more firm safeguards of national security throughout the inter-war years. The fifteen-year occupation of the Rhineland proved equally illusory: it meant that allied forces would be withdrawn just after the interval of time which Germany needed to revive her ambitions and regain her military strength. It can certainly be contended that the material securities exacted from Germany were in these ways too slight.

On the other hand, the attempts to insist on German acceptance of the so-called War Guilt Clause were quite unrealistic. A sense of moral responsibility could not be created by including a statement of it in a document which German representatives were compelled to sign: and the demand for reparations for war-damage inflicted by the German armies, which was made to hinge upon this statement, was pitched in astronomical figures without any serious consideration of how it would be economically possible for Germany to pay or for the Allies to receive such wealth. No figure of reparations was fixed in the Treaty, although vast claims were made by France, Belgium, and Britain. A Reparations Commission was set up to fix the amount to be demanded and to arrange for the methods and time of payment. In this way the unavoidable difficulties were shelved, and left to be a recurrent source of rancour during the next decade. Immediately, however, other forms of reparation were exacted. Germany was deprived of all her colonial possessions, most of her fleet and the bulk of her merchant marine, as well as of property owned by German citizens abroad. The fleet was mostly scuttled by its crews at Scapa Flow. Military conscription in Germany was forbidden, and her army was limited to 100,000 men. She was forbidden to have heavy artillery, aviation, or submarines. She could not have afforded to build such weapons anyhow for some years after the war, and by the time she could afford them there were ample ways of evading the watchfulness of disarmament commissions. Meanwhile, since her small army had to be a voluntarily recruited and professional army, the power of the officer caste was preserved and it was allowed to plan the rapid expansion of German military strength as soon as possible. This whole series of punitive and compensatory measures was ill-devised and impracticable. They served to consolidate German national resentment without taking any watertight securities against her capacity to express that resentment in action.

The settlement in eastern Europe, embodied in the four other treaties drafted and concluded by the conference, was mainly concerned with redrawing the political map and seeking some protection for the national minorities which, even after the most ingenious map-drawing, were still left on the wrong sides of frontiers. It was here that endless compromises and refinements had to be made in applying the doctrine of 'national self-determination'. The Southern Slav movement was broadly satisfied by the amalgamation of Serbia, Slovenia, and Croatia into Yugoslavia, although Italy, as promised in the secret treaty of 1915, was given Trieste and some Dalmatian islands. Poland was reconstituted as an independent state, and was given an outlet to the sea through the 'Polish Corridor' of Posen and West Prussia. These areas contained German minorities and their bestowal upon Poland had the effect of separating East Prussia from the rest of

Germany. Rumania was enlarged by the addition of former Russian and Hungarian territories. Greece was enlarged at the expense of Turkey. A new composite republic was created in Czechoslovakia, including Czechs, Slovaks, Ruthenians, and Sudeten Germans. The Baltic nations of Finland, Latvia, Lithuania, and Estonia were recognized as independent states. Austria and Hungary became tiny landlocked and separated states. Turkey eventually became a strong new state under Mustapha Kemal, but confined to Constantinople and Asia Minor. Syria and Lebanon were entrusted to French administration, and Palestine, Transjordan, and Iraq to British, as mandated territories. This meant that they were administered by these countries who were responsible for them to the newly set up Permanent Mandates Commission of the League of Nations. Former German colonial possessions were distributed on a similar basis, German South-West Africa going to the Union of South Africa, her other African colonies being divided between Britain, France, and Belgium. The northern Pacific islands were mandated to Japan, German New Guinea to Australia, and German Samoa to New Zealand.

Criticism of the wisdom of these arrangements must be distinguished from criticism of the peacemakers at Paris. There were many matters in which they had no real choice. Before they met the new states of eastern Europe were in existence, and the most that could be done in Paris was to ensure that the new frontiers should be reasonable ones. Similarly, the powers concerned were already in occupation of the territories now

mandated to them, and to stipulate the conditions under
which they should be administered was the most that
the conference could do. They could not have restored
the pre-war Empires even had they wished to do so,
because they had utterly disintegrated. Nor can the
peacemakers be blamed for the continuance of large
and troublesome national minorities in eastern Europe.
There were now fewer people living under what they
felt to be an alien rule than there were before. The
novelty was that the roles were usually now reversed,
and it was Germans and Hungarians who lived as
minorities under Polish, Czech, or Italian rule. Benefit
of the doubt might more often have been given to the
defeated nationalities, but otherwise things could have
been arranged little differently. The systematic trans-
planting of minorities to different sides of the frontiers
was rightly ruled out as bringing more suffering and
hardship to a war-stricken area: though some migrated
spontaneously, and the flight of Greek minorities from
Turkey and the removal of Turkish minorities from
Greece in 1923 served this purpose. There was nothing
inherently unjust in leaving peoples of different nationality within one state, so long as they were then treated
with justice by the dominant majority of that state.
The succession states, as the new creations were called,
signed treaties with the allied powers undertaking that
national minorities would not be subjected to dis-
abilities: though this well-meant device, giving an
aggrieved minority the right to petition against its
government to an external authority which had little
means at its disposal to protect them, did not prove to

be a good way of reconciling groups within a multi-national state.

Most attacks upon the settlement during the following twenty years arose from the disparity between the excessively high hopes that men had pinned upon it and its tangle of uninspiring compromises. Yet these compromises inevitably arose in any attempt to apply rational or moral principles to the fragmented territories of Europe. Justice in such matters could never be other than relative: yet the mood of men was perfectionist. It was simply impossible to satisfy the needs of Poland for an outlet to the Baltic down the Vistula and at the same time the demands of Germans that East Prussia must not be territorially separated from Germany. There was no satisfactory impartial solution to the rival claims of Jews and Arabs in Palestine. There was no humane way to remove the minorities problem from Balkan politics. Such conflicts of national interest have always been solved, in the end, by the use of force or by a long process of habituation and healing which makes them cease to matter. They could not be solved, in terms of absolute justice, by a single peace conference. Yet that was just what the peacemakers of Paris were, by so many, expected to achieve. Considering the passions aroused by more than four years of war, the intractability of the problems themselves, and the unknown aftermath looming ahead, the makers of the settlement achieved more than should have seemed probable when they first met.

§4. *Social Repercussions*

The most important single consequence of the war
on society was a strengthening of the sentiments and
passions of nationalism, of which the principles of
national self-determination applied in the settlement
were only a reflection. The mass mobilizations and
losses, the bitter passions aroused by the massacre of
ten million men, the prolonged strain of sustained war
effort, the sharing of sorrows in adversity and of triumph in victory, all conspired to besiege men's minds
with nationalist pride and patriotic fervour. In each
country the enemy was depicted as bestial, unscrupu-
lous, and entirely hateful. From the outset nationalism had proved to be a much stronger force than
socialism. By all save a few extreme revolutionaries the
Marxist theses that the working men of all countries
had nothing to lose but their economic chains, that
wars were capitalist wars in which workers should take
no part, were completely abandoned. In each country,
in 1914, the parliamentary socialist parties supported
their national governments and voted for mobilization
and war-credits. The war, save latterly in Russia, was
not paralysed by strikes and pacifist sabotage. It was
left to a few individual socialists or pacifists to resist the
war effort, but socialism in the main became a national
socialism.[1] This alliance of the two strongest move-

[1] The symbol of the future split was the 'Zimmerwald
programme' of 1915, when the anti-war socialist minority
groups from each country met together and formulated the
demand for immediate peace without annexations or indemni-
ties. Lenin was especially active in this movement, the
embryo of the future Comintern.

ments in the modern world, in various other forms, was to haunt all the subsequent years. The triumph of the extremist group in Russia in 1917 widened and perpetuated the split within the socialist ranks. Parliamentary socialists could not accept the brutal methods of Bolshevism any more than they had been able to sustain the class-war theses of Marxism. Henceforth communism and socialism parted company, although it took events of the next decade to clarify and widen the divergence.

The strengthening of nationalism and of the nationalist kind of socialism was accompanied by what might be called the nationalizing of capitalism. Each government had to assume a high degree of control and direction over the whole economic life of its country. Foreign trade and investment had to be controlled, agricultural and industrial production had to be planned or directed to meet the demands for mobilization and war-supplies. Production for civilian use and for non-essentials had to be pruned, supplies of raw materials had to be secured, and the manpower (and increasingly womanpower too) of each nation had to be directed. Capitalists who exploited shortages or who made too much out of war-contracts became bitterly hated as 'profiteers': and the ever-increasing burden of taxation tended to level incomes and to put immense new power into the hands of governments. Machinery for achieving all these purposes, as well as for the rationing of foodstuffs and control of prices, was set up by each state. It brought new problems of administration, bureaucratic powers, and management. Because the United States entered the war late and her expanding economy made it less necessary, this process went much less far there than in the European countries, but there too it made some headway. Her relationship to Europe was also revolutionized by the war. British and French citizens and companies had held huge investments in the United States, as had other Europeans. In 1914 these had amounted to some £800 millions. During the war their governments took over these investments and sold them in America to buy supplies, compensating their owners in pounds or francs. In addition European governments raised vast war-loans in America. As a result, the United States emerged from the war as the world's greatest creditor, to whom European countries owed nearly £2,000 millions. Repayment of these war-debts was to remain a thorny problem in the next decade.

The social upheavals caused by the war were enormous. The normal balance of age-groups and of sexes in the population was upset, because family life was disrupted during mobilization, millions of young men were killed, and the birth-rate fell sharply only to rise equally sharply after war ended. Women, patriotically working in war factories and services, entered the labour-market on a scale unknown before. Finding thereby an economic basis for greater independence, many remained in it. Their role in the war effort, especially in Britain, made their demands for the vote irresistible after the war. Throughout the world the changing status of women in the community is one of the more silent and unnoticed revolutions of modern

times. From a status of at worst legal and social subservience, at best economic and political dependence,
women have in one country after another gained a position of greater equality with men. This revolution has
extended even to Asia, and is likely eventually to affect
Africa. In the whole process in Britain and western
Europe the war played an important part. Further social
repercussions followed from the post-war inflation of
prices and from the burden of heavy taxation. All whose
living depended on fixed incomes from investments,
pensions, or savings, or whose money-wages could not
easily be raised, suffered a decline in their standard of
life. The strains and hardships, the hysteria and ex-
haustion of war left emotionally overwrought and un-
balanced nations to grapple with its aftermath.

Above all, the economic relationship between
Europe and the other continents was revolutionized.
In the pre-war world every advanced European country
had imported more than it exported, paying for the
balance with interest on its foreign investments, and
with shipping or other services. Their high standard of
living had depended on this. Now European countries,
in order to pay war-debts and recover their foreign
trade in a period of rising prices, had to try to export
more goods than they imported. Their standards of
living correspondingly suffered. In the pre-war world,
as depicted above, industrial production had centred
upon Europe and the bulk of its imports from other
continents had been raw materials and foodstuffs. Non-
European countries had, in the main, depended on
Europe's exports for their finished goods, just as they

G

depended on its investments for their capital and on its
emigrants for their technical skills. This organic interdependence, involving a privileged position for European countries *vis-à-vis* the rest, had been partially
undermined by 1914: but the rapid industrial expansion of the United States, the Dominions, Japan, and
some of the South American states to meet the in-
satiable war-time demands for supplies removed for
ever the privileged industrial position of Europe. The
overseas countries now joined the ranks of international
exporters of manufactured goods, or were able to meet
a higher proportion of their own domestic needs. New
commercial relations had been established which left
European countries out of account. The United States
traded more directly with South America and the Far
East. Japan traded more directly with South America,
Australasia, and India. Europe was still one of the
greatest industrial centres of the world: she was no
longer the focus of industrial production. She was to
some extent, during the next two decades, able to re-
establish her position in the world. But she could never
recapture the privileged heights of 1914. Just as the
balance of economic advantages had shifted, before
1914, as between one European power and another, so
now it shifted as between the continents, and all the
European powers suffered a relative decline in world
importance.

.   .   .   .   .

These changes and their revolutionary characte
were not fully perceived in 1919. The immediate prac
tical problems of recovering from the devastations an

dislocations of war were too urgent. But three things loomed large in men's minds at that time. The first was the triumph of democracy. It was the old dynasties which had gone down in defeat and collapse, the western democratic states which had survived in victory. Moreover, the new states with very few exceptions adopted highly democratic constitutions: even Germany. The world really seemed to have been made safe for democracy. This was more apparent and seemed more important than the triumphs of nationalism. Secondly, there was the League of Nations and its accompaniments—the High Court of International Justice at the Hague, the International Labour Organization, the Permanent Mandates Commission, the Minorities Commission. Herein lay the hope of the future for a more rational and peaceful international order, the remedy for that so-called 'international anarchy' of 1914 which, many believed, had produced the war. Within the Assembly of the League and its Council, representing the logical extension of liberal democratic principles to international organization, the nations of the world could meet and remove those obstacles to their good relationships and prosperity which had in the past caused wars. President Wilson succeeded in getting the Covenant of the League included in the texts of all the treaties, so it was thoroughly woven into the fabric of the peace settlement. Other governments, especially the French and the British, were at first sceptical of its merits. But each began to believe that it could serve some of its national interests through the League, and learned to support

and use it. It suffered a tremendous blow when the
United States Senate, refusing to ratify the Treaties,
kept the United States from joining the League. Its
prime sponsor had deserted it. Since its Assembly represented national governments and the succession
states regarded it as part of the whole settlement to
which they owed their official existence it drew on new
sources of enthusiasm and support. During the next
decade, as the problems of post-war reconstruction
pressed hard on all countries, a certain *mystique* of the
League grew up in western Europe. It seemed the only
life-line to a more hopeful future. Yet in those very
years it was being undermined by other forces, ultra-
nationalist and warlike, which in the end were to destroy it. Thirdly, there was Bolshevism. That loomed
perhaps larger in men's minds and fears in 1919 than
anything else in the post-war world. The cordon of new
states in the eastern marchlands was welcomed by the
west as a barrier against the spread of this new terror.
Here the peacemakers of 1919 were correct in their
diagnosis, though futile in their remedies. Here, indeed,
was the most momentous political phenomenon of the
post-war world.

Chapter Three

POST-WAR DECADE, 1919–1929

§1. *Schism in Socialism*

DURING the last quarter of the nineteenth century socialist movements in every advanced country were faced with a crucial decision. Should they adhere to strict Marxist doctrine, and so aim at overthrowing the state and replacing it by a new proletarian state? Or should they set out to capture the existing state, take it over as a working régime, and use it to achieve socialistic reforms? This issue split socialist movements in most countries into revolutionary and participationist sections. Wherever there existed a wide franchise, a well-developed industrial system, and a strong trade union movement there were strong inducements to seek power by parliamentary and constitutional means. This happened, in general, in the United Kingdom, France, Germany, and Scandinavia. The socialists who chose this course had to set about either winning a majority of the electorate to their cause, or joining with other parliamentary parties to secure a share in government. In either event, they had to place before the electorate not only their ultimate objectives and basic doctrines, but an immediate programme of practical reforms which could be attained within the existing social and economic framework. Once committed to democratic and constitutional methods of procedure, they tended to become increasingly democratic in temper and behaviour. In countries where the franchise was still narrow, as in Italy before 1913 and Belgium and Holland before 1918, socialists went on using the more revolutionary language and methods of Marxism longer than their colleagues in Britain or France. But Marxism remained most meaningful where a degree of industrialization co-existed with the absence of any working machinery for constitutional government: as in Russia after the patent failure of the Duma of 1905. There was, in this way, a close correlation between the earlier successes of liberal democracy and the growth of parliamentary socialism: and the cleavage between social democracy in western Europe and communist totalitarianism in eastern Europe originates in this correlation.

The divergence which showed itself clearly in the Zimmerwald Programme of 1915 was hardened by the successful Bolshevik Revolution of 1917. The Russian Social Democratic Labour Party had, in 1903, debated this very issue. The wing which held that the party must be revolutionary, and so must be tightly organized round a hard core of reliable and carefully chosen revolutionaries, directing party activities through a small central committee not answerable to the rank and file members, was led by Lenin. It gained the day, against the looser and more democratic conception of party organization which would have weakened the party as an instrument of revolution. In 1912 the party split over this issue, and the Leninist Bolshevik Party thereafter existed in readiness to seize the revolutionary opportunities offered by the failures of the Tsarist régime.

The roots of the revolutionary situation in Russia

lay in its highly despotic, harsh, and corrupt system of government, its backward economic life, and the fermentation in these conditions of ideals derived from the French Revolution of 1789, as well as from Marxism. The first fruits of this fermentation had been admirable. They included the novels of Tolstoy and Dostoievsky, the music of Tchaikovsky and Rimsky-Korsakov. Russian culture in the later nineteenth century had merged into European culture more completely than ever before, and at the same time western industrial methods were penetrating western Russia. Railways, telegraphs, factories, foreign investments, foreign trade, were increasingly linking Russia with the rest of Europe. In 1905 when the Tsar Nicholas II summoned the Duma it seemed that she was coming still more within the pattern of western civilization. For the next decade she had the appearances of at least a semi-constitutional monarchy. But the Duma enjoyed no real powers, and liberal constitutionalism struck no deep roots in Russian soil.

Lenin proved to be the greatest revolutionary genius of the modern world, and one of the greatest of all time. He combined remarkable powers of intellectual analysis and a fanatical faith in the rightness of his conclusions with an acute sense of political realities and of practical statecraft. He used this rare combination of unusual powers to weld his party into an irresistible weapon of revolutionary action. Through it, he twisted the whole development of Russia into a new channel, which made it increasingly divergent from the rest of Europe. He quite literally changed the course of world history.

Yet Lenin and the Bolshevik Party did little or nothing to produce revolution in Russia. The situation of 1917 arose from quite other causes: from the bankruptcy of the old régime and the breakdown of government produced by three years of war. The successful conduct of modern war called for national solidarity and self-confidence as well as for efficiency of governmental direction, neither of which Russia of the Tsars possessed. When revolution broke out in March 1917 the Bolshevik leaders were taken more by surprise than the government itself. They were mostly in exile abroad. An emergency committee of the Duma and the newly created Soviet of Workers' and Soldiers' Deputies in Petrograd set up a provisional liberal government under Prince Lvov. When the Tsar was compelled to abdicate on 17 March, a republic was proclaimed.

The provisional government, sharing most of the political ideals of the western allies and hoping to establish a constitutional democratic régime in Russia, continued the war against Germany. In April the German government, knowing that the Bolshevik leaders stood for making peace with Germany, offered them a safe passage from Switzerland to Russia through Germany in a sealed train. This was the second service rendered by the German High Command to the cause of Bolshevism: the first had been to inflict such heavy losses on Russia. Now Lenin, back in Russia, could refine his revolutionary weapon ready for timely seizure of power. The new government soon found that it could not sustain both war and revolution at the same time. It proclaimed a distribution of land to the peasants. The Russian armies simply dissolved, as the peasant-soldiers went home to make sure of getting the land. Confusion and administrative chaos had gone too far for the situation to be saved. On the night of 6 November the Bolsheviks took over power. Their main agents were the Petrograd Soviet, units of the army and navy, and the party organization itself. The Bolshevik Revolution, in its initial stage, was a *coup d'état* amidst chaos. Its programme, formulated by Lenin, was fourfold: land to the peasants; food to the starving; power to the Soviets; and peace with Germany. The first was already happening, and the last was soon accomplished in the Treaty of Brest-Litovsk. The second and third were achieved together, in that food was distributed only to those willing to grant power to the Soviets. Soviets or workers' councils sprang up all over the country, especially in factories and army units, under the auspices of the party. Thus power was in fact wielded by the highly disciplined and admirably organized party which Lenin had been forging since 1903. Its power was immediately consolidated by the creation of two further organizations: the 'Extraordinary All-Russian Commission of Struggle against Counter-Revolution, Speculation, and Sabotage', more briefly known as the CHEKA, and subsequently as OGPU, NKVD, and MVD; and a month later in January 1918 the Red Army was founded by Trotsky. In this way the four main organs of the Bolshevik political system were set up within the first three months. With these four instruments of the party (in March 1918 re-christened the Communist Party), the

Soviets, the secret police, and the Red Army, Lenin proceeded to erect the first of the totalitarian single-party dictatorships of the modern world.

.   .   .   .   .

Every subsequent phase of the revolution in Russia moved, from the viewpoint of world history, in one direction: towards the fusion of communism with nationalism. The period of foreign intervention, which continued until 1922, served to consolidate the power of the party as a national government. It forged the Red Army into a more efficient fighting force for national defence. Its triumph over the mixed forces of counter-revolutionaries and British, French, United States, and Japanese contingents, left the party and its instruments without serious armed and organized opposition. On the home front the CHEKA launched a reign of terror which far exceeded, in brutality and bloodshed, the classical reign of terror in France in 1793. By ruthlessness and massacre it succeeded in destroying all elements of 'bourgeois' reaction, and eliminated all rivals to the Bolsheviks among the other revolutionary movements. By 1922 the Communist Party of Lenin enjoyed complete and undisputed dictatorship over the whole of Russia up to the western borders fixed by the Paris Conference.

The period of Lenin's New Economic Policy (1921–7) helped to heal some of the wounds which hasty revolutionary action had opened. It was, in his own words, taking 'two steps forward, one step back,' and by his skill in checking a great social revolution in midstream and deliberately controlling its direction he

showed how complete was the mastery of the party over
the course of Russian development. The critics of this
policy, including Trotsky, could point to the return of
bourgeois habits, private property, the class of 'new
rich' and disillusionment about collectivization. But
the state still controlled all the major means of production. Lenin's successor as secretary of the party, the
Georgian Joseph Stalin, was able to show how it could
now proceed to long-term economic planning. The
triumph of Stalin, who favoured the goal of 'socialism
in a single state' as against his Trotskyite critics
who favoured the immediate goal of 'permanent' world
revolution, was a triumph of nationalism over international communism. Trotsky was exiled to Siberia,
and after living in Turkey, France, and Mexico was
murdered in 1940. His followers were discredited and
purged from the party during the nineteen-thirties.
Stalin proceeded, after 1928, with his series of Five-
Year Plans designed to equip Russia with heavy industry and better transport, to mechanize and collectivize
agriculture, and to develop new sources of power and
industry beyond the Urals.[1] Detailed economic planning had not been visualized in 1917, and indeed since
Marxist doctrine presupposed that the economic structure of society determined the political structure, state
planning of economic life had been at first looked upon
as an inversion of the normal process of history. But
under Stalin's rule it became and remained a permanent

---

[1] The first Five-Year Plan was launched in 1928, the
second in 1932, a third was interrupted by the second World
War, and a fourth, between 1946 and 1950, was devoted to
post-war reconstruction.

characteristic of Communist government in Russia. The effect was to produce throughout the whole territory a highly integrated national economy, and to weld its citizens into a more consciously united community than ever before in their history.

Taken together, the Plans have been Russia's industrial revolution. In two decades they have accomplished what has taken several decades in other countries. By 1939, four-fifths of her industrial production came from plants built during the previous ten years. As many of these were situated east of the Urals, the Plans carried modern industrialization far into the heart of Asia. They opened up the vast mineral resources of central Asia, and so added enormously to the stock of the world's available wealth. Russia, economically as well as politically, became more a part of Asia than a part of Europe. Her example stimulated the demand of other Asiatic peoples, particularly China and India, for comparable industrialization. The social transformation effected in the peoples of the Soviet Union was incalculable. There came into being a great new class of bureaucrats, managers, engineers, and technicians such as Russia had never before known. It is they who enjoy the greatest social prestige and advantages. At the same time, by mechanization and more scientific development of agriculture, the Plans enabled the soil of Russia to sustain a greatly increased population at a higher standard of living. Although in productive efficiency, and in *per capita* output, Russia still lags behind the United States, it was these tremendous changes in her economy which made her, by the middle of the twentieth century, the chief rival to the United States as a world power.

The attitude of the European powers to this new phenomenon passed through various phases in the nineteen-twenties. At first the revolution and the terror provoked a violent reaction of revulsion and fear. The first power to make a formal agreement with Russia was, characteristically enough, Germany. By the Treaty of Rapallo in 1922 both the ostracised powers gained advantages. Russia gained diplomatic recognition, German manufactures and technical help. Germany gained a market and the opportunity for her military officers and technicians to keep in good training by helping Russia. It was the third time that Germany had given substantial and timely aid to the Bolshevik Party. Gradually, during the next decade, the Soviet Union made trade agreements with other western countries, and in 1934 she was admitted to membership of the League of Nations. But her relations with the west were periodically disturbed by the activities of the Comintern, created in March 1919, which the Russians insisted held no official status. Its activities usually chimed remarkably well with the purposes of Soviet foreign policy. She was in truth following a double policy: for some purposes, operating on the principle that her task was to achieve communism in a single country first; for others, adhering to the principle that world revolution must remain the inevitable goal of communism, so that no opportunity should be missed to promote this end. As will be seen, the chief fruit of this policy in the nineteen-thirties was the growth of fascist and other powerful anti-communist movements in most western countries. These movements prospered before communism had gained any firm foothold in those countries, so that it was invariably the loser.

By 1932, when the first Five-Year Plan was completed, the major effects of the Bolshevik Revolution, together with the post-war settlement, had been to push Russia more out of Europe and more into Asia. Both the creed of Marxism which she adopted, and the methods of industrialization she used, were made in western Europe. But in Russia they produced quite novel repercussions. A powerful monolithic party dictatorship, a highly integrated planned national economy, a dynamic movement aiming at world revolution, had not accompanied the industrialization of any other country. Industrialism in Asia was henceforth to be tied to very different political forces from industrialism in Europe or in the United States.

The most important achievement of the Bolshevik Revolution for world history was that it established 'socialism in a single state', and linked communism in that state with the deep-rooted sentiments and traditions of Russian nationalism. It was significant that the Bolshevik Party extended its power over a territory as vast as the whole of Russia—a sixth of the earth's land surface. Soviet forces occupied Azerbaidjan, Armenia, and Georgia in 1920–1921 and Mongolia in 1922. But it was no less significant that there, until 1940, the expansions of Bolshevik power ended. They failed in Latvia in 1919. In the same year an abortive communist régime in Hungary, headed by Béla Kun, was over-

thrown within six months. Communist attempts to
seize power failed in Germany in 1921 and 1923, in
Bulgaria in 1923, in China in 1927, in Spain during the
Popular Front government. The confinement of the
communist régime to Russian territories until after
1940 was of momentous importance, because it compelled communism to adapt itself to survival in a single
country surrounded by non-communist states. It thus
made necessary an alliance, and eventually a fusion,
between the forces and ideas of nationalism and of communism. This alliance was elaborated and consolidated
by the achievements of the Five Year Plans, by the cult
of Stalin as a great Russian national hero, and by the
experience of sustained national resistance to German
invasion after 1941. The next successful communist
régime, in Yugoslavia, was not established until 1944
and was then so nationalistic in character that it defied
the directives of the Kremlin. Meanwhile democratic
socialism, by increasing participation in parliamentary
life in the nations of western Europe, was also becoming
more nationalistic in character. Throughout the world
after 1919 the schism in socialism widened: and each
wing of the movement tended to merge with the forces
of nationalism.[1]

§2. *International Organization*

The Covenant of the League of Nations created the

[1] See further below, Chapter IV, §2. The only good analysis,
on a world scale, of social conditions which have helped or
hindered communist revolutionary activity, is in H. Seton-
Watson: *The Pattern of Communist Revolution: An Historical
Analysis* (1953).

most elaborate and most nearly world-wide international organization hitherto set up. But it always fell far short of being universal, and this proved to be one of its fatal defects. From the start Russia was excluded, and so was Germany; the United States excluded itself. With three of the world's greatest powers outside its walls the League was fatally weakened. Its effectiveness now depended essentially on a working partnership between France and the British Commonwealth. In 1933 it was further weakened by the withdrawal of Japan, although Germany had meanwhile been admitted in 1926. By the time the Soviet Union was admitted in 1934, Germany had left it. Even apart from the permanent absence of the United States, there was no moment when all the great European powers were simultaneously members of it. It was never fully a world organization, despite the piecemeal participation of the United States with many of its more technical activities, and with the International Labour Organization.

Because of the exclusion of the powers most dissatisfied with the settlement, and because of the inclusion of the Covenant in the peace treaties themselves, the League was from the first identified with preservation of the settlement. Wilson's consoling hope that shortcomings of the settlement would be remedied through the League was therefore doomed to disappointment. The League did not prove to be a suitable instrument for what came to be known as 'peaceful change'. The succession states particularly, reinforced by France, tended to look upon any proposed change in the settlement as a weakening of the very basis for their survival. As they were solidly within the League the whole time, their weight was decisive in blocking any important modifications of the settlement by concerted agreement through the League. It became increasingly certain and obvious that any substantial modifications would come in defiance of the League, and therefore by violence. That aspect of the League which made it a concert of European powers for maintaining the *status quo* came to predominate over its ecumenical aspects, as a world-wide agency for international conciliation.

At the same time, some of the basic assumptions which had made the structure of the League appear a reasonable and hopeful one in 1919 soon began to dissolve. The institution of the General Assembly, in which each member state was equally represented and in which unanimity was required for all important decisions, made sense so long as it was assumed that democracy would be the common pattern of at least most states in modern Europe; and that they would be sufficiently like-minded to hold to the general principles and ideals of democracy and to want peace. One of the postulates of liberal thought in 1919 was that democratic peoples would be peace-loving, and would have a positive urge to organize a peaceful order. This postulate was itself a fallacy, and a relic of the over-intellectualist thinking of nineteenth-century liberalism. Moreover, despite the popularity of democratic constitutions in Europe, there was, after 1922, the large and decisive exception of Fascist Italy. Even governments ostensibly democratic in basis and purpose began to pursue far from peaceful or liberal ends. When

H

nationalist rivalries and jealousies, strengthened rather
than weakened by the war and by the settlement, began
to dominate international relations, the League ma
chinery became the apotheosis not of liberal democracy
but of nationalism. The principles of equal representa
tion of all states and of unanimous voting became the
sanctification of separatist national sovereignty. It i
true that the Covenant would hardly have been
accepted and approved in 1919 had these provisions for
preserving national sovereignty not been included: but
the falsity of the assumption that liberal democracy
would now triumph in the world destroyed the only co
hesive force which might conceivably have transcended
nationalism. When that assumption proved unfounded
all that was left was the paradox of an international
machine operating on a basis of atomistic nationalism
as well as of a world organization that was not world-
wide. It was neither universal enough to achieve general
conciliation, nor cohesive enough to achieve decisive
action as a concert of powers.

It was precisely when these facts had become irrefut
able that there grew up, in the public opinion of many
countries, an internationalist *mystique* which looked to
the League and its affiliated organizations to perform
miracles. The peoples of nearly all former belligerents
experienced a profound revulsion against war, and be
came convinced that another world war would spell the
destruction of civilization. Pacifist sentiments and
theories abounded among liberal-minded people in
Britain, France, Scandinavia, and the United States. I
came to be felt that war must be avoided at all costs

and the new international organizations seemed to be the only means, other than an absolute pacifism, by which to promote peace. When Bolshevism in Russia preached the inevitability of capitalist wars, when Mussolini in Italy was exalting war as a force of purification and invigoration for a people who aspired to greater power, when Germany was secretly re-arming with help from Russia, the western powers on whose resolution the success of the League depended were infused with a spirit of pacifism and defeatism. Internationalism, in the sense of a resolve to remain strong enough to enforce those guarantees of 'collective security' enshrined in Articles 16 and 17 of the Covenant, became utterly confused with pacifism, in the sense of a refusal to contemplate action by armed force, even to defend a member of the League from aggression. Prompted partly by economic needs, partly by pressures from pacifist opinion, and partly by inertia, the governments of the western powers allowed themselves to disarm. Since the Covenant provided for no unified armed force, but relied entirely upon the concerted use of national armaments to restrain or resist aggression, the League was robbed of its resources of military strength just when the military might of the most probable aggressors was accumulating and just when large sections of public opinion pinned their greatest hopes of security on action by the League. The temptations placed before a potential aggressor were thus at their greatest, when the only hope of successfully deterring him was to keep such temptations at the minimum.

Sensing the inadequacies of the League, of which France had from the first been most acutely aware, the powers entered into a series of separate and supplementary agreements and treaties, designed to buttress the League or to yield them separate security should the League fail. The French turned first to the succession states, whose interests were most in harmony with those of France. They formed an alliance with Poland in 1921 and then with the Little Entente of Czechoslovakia, Yugoslavia, and Rumania. In 1925 the 'spirit of Locarno' produced treaties by which in effect Germany guaranteed the frontiers of Belgium and France, and undertook to resort only to agreement or arbitration to change her frontiers with Poland and Czechoslovakia. Britain guaranteed the frontiers between Germany and France and between Germany and Belgium; and for three years there seemed to be a new hope of permanent settlement in Europe. In 1926 Germany was admitted to the League. The United States and France took the initiative in formulating the Briand-Kellogg Pact of 1928, by which the signatories renounced war as an instrument of national policy or—as the phrase was—they 'outlawed war'. It was signed by most states in the world. The notion that war can be thus signed out of existence when there are militant and aggressive governments in the world was the culmination of this phase of idealistic and perfectionist thinking about international relations.[1] In 1930 M. Briand circulated a

[1] But with the efforts to revive the older distinction between just and unjust wars, and to define 'crimes against peace' at the Nuremberg Trials, the Kellogg Pact may now have renewed significance. See below, Chapter V, §1.

proposal for what was misleadingly called 'European Federal Union', but which in fact was a still further form of multilateral regional agreement. But by then economic forces, rather than political, had taken charge of world affairs, and in Germany 107 National Socialists were elected to the Reichstag. The honeymoon between France and Germany was over. It had rested unfortunately on temporary factors—on the genuine reluctance of both governments to contemplate war, on the personal *rapports* between men like Arthur Henderson, Ramsay MacDonald and Sir Austen Chamberlain in Britain, Aristide Briand and Édouard Herriot in France and Gustav Stresemann in Germany, on the pressure of anti-war sentiments in all three countries. But these forces were too transient to counteract the powerfully disruptive and separatist forces in Europe: the greatest of which were nationalistic fear and pride. Economic dislocations and upheavals were exacerbating both. Germany, in particular, suffered sharp inflation which, after the French occupation of the Ruhr in 1923, culminated in a catastrophic currency collapse. It was a much more profound revolution than that of 1918, for the large middle and professional classes in Germany were ruined as savings and pensions became worthless. It was from this social revolution, even more than from the defeat of 1918, that the forces of Hitlerism were to draw their strength.

.   .   .   .   .

Meanwhile the 'Far Eastern Question', in many ways reminiscent of the problems which had combined to create the nineteenth-century Eastern Question, had entered upon a new phase. The component elements were a weak and unstable China, a new and dynamic Russia, and an expanding and aggressive Japan. The Chinese Revolution of 1911, which had aimed at the expulsion of both Manchu rulers and foreigners, had only partially succeeded, and had left China a prey to internal strife. In 1922 civil war ravaged the northern and central provinces and the following year Dr. Sun Yat-sen, president of the Kuomintang nationalist party, established himself as head of the government at Canton, in the south. The Kuomintang, led by young Chinese intellectuals who had imbibed western ideas of self-determination, were much impressed by the Bolshevik Revolution, and Dr. Sun Yat-sen took as his chief adviser a Russian, Borodin. There grew up a strong communist section of the party, and because Borodin's influence was directed towards driving out the western powers from their concessions in China, it became possible to blend Chinese nationalism with Soviet aims of world revolution.[1] The Russian and Chinese Revolutions were depicted as twin facets of one world-wide movement of liberation from the bonds of western capitalism. Just as Germany sent advisers and technicians to Russia, so the Russians sent advisers and technicians to China. With a common frontier of 4,000 miles, Russian influence in China was inevitably very great. The extent of British interests in China made her

[1] Dr. Sun Yat-sen's 'Three People's Principles', the official ideology of the Chinese Revolution, may be roughly translated as 'Nationalism, Socialism, Democracy', and were an adaptation to Chinese conditions of western European ideals

the main target for nationalist grievances, and incidents at Shanghai and Canton in 1925 led to a boycott of British goods, of which the chief beneficiary was Japan.

But by 1927 the scene changed. Britain, awakening to the force of Chinese nationalism, adopted a policy of conciliation. It transferred the concession at Hankow to China and the nationalist government established itself there, as being a more central capital. There appeared a split between the more revolutionary wing of the Kuomintang, adhering to Soviet affiliations, and the right wing which found a new and vigorous leader in General Chiang Kai-shek. Chiang set up a rival government at Nanking, succeeded in expelling Borodin and the other Russian advisers, and then transferred the seat of the national government to Nanking. Although this government enjoyed only weak control or none at all in the outlying provinces, and communism was still strong in some of the central provinces, British interests were served by the existence of a more orderly country with which to trade. On the other hand, Japan took alarm at this prospect of a stronger and more united China. With Russian influences diminished, she hoped to renew that expansion into China which she had been compelled to forego since 1921. The Soviet Union was increasingly absorbed in her internal Five-Year Plans from 1928 onwards. Japanese policy fell into the hands of the more militaristic elements, who planned to secure Japanese ascendancy in China. The only forces which might have restrained it were the external powers of Britain and the

United States: but these had been largely neutralized by the Washington Agreements about naval power in 1921, and by the failure of the United States to adopt any firm or clear policy towards Japanese expansion in the Far East. Japan, strongly fortified by her economic gains during the war and by her territorial gains in the peace settlement, felt that the moment had come to enlarge her grip over Manchuria and northern China. This campaign of expansion was to begin in 1931 with her occupation of all Manchuria and the invasion of Shanghai and much of northern China. The Chinese, deeply divided and disorganized, were in no condition to resist effectively. Although war was not formally declared, China remained in a state of hostilities with Japan from 1931 until the Japanese defeat in 1945.

The ultimate importance of this revolution in the balance of power in the Pacific and the Far East was hidden until after the second world war. But the immediate consequence was the discredit of the new international security organization of the League of Nations. When China appealed to the League in 1931 it was the first test of that organization's ability to handle an issue involving open aggression of one major power against another.[1] The League sent a Commission under Lord Lytton to report on the situation. The report avoided any suggestion that sanctions, under

[1] With his bombardment of Corfu and his extraction of an indemnity from Greece in 1923, Mussolini had already successfully forced the powers to act through the Ambassadors' Conference rather than through the League and the International Court: but then one party had been a small power. Corfu was, however, an omen of things to come.

Article 16, should be invoked, and the leading members of the League refused to take any military action to aid China. They indeed accepted a solution which left the Japanese in occupation of Manchuria and north-east China. Henceforth, it was concluded, the League was utterly unreliable as a provider of security, however valuable might be its other activities in promoting international co-operation about preventing trade in white slaves or narcotics. It had suffered its first serious blow as an instrument for preventing aggression or war, and the pre-1914 international anarchy had virtually returned.

These developments of the nineteen-twenties left international organization in a confused and incoherent condition. At an unofficial or semi-official level the patient constructive co-operation of the late nineteenth century continued. The ideals and habits of mind which had produced the International Red Cross, the International Federation of Trade Unions, the Boy Scout movement, and four or five hundred similar voluntary bodies continued unabated. It was calculated that an average of a hundred international conferences were held each year, and the role of such activities in weaving the fabric of a real international society cannot be overlooked. As an English writer put it in 1932,

A survey of international society would show it to be composed not only of the intercourse of each state with every other state, but of the collaboration of doctors, statisticians, trade-unionists, hotel-keepers, boy-scouts, chambers of commerce, parliamentarians, and innumerable specialists drawn from almost every country of the world into an association not as nationals of their countries but as representatives of a special occupation or interest.[1]

Even much of the co-operation at a more official level was concerned with extending former conventions about postal, telegraphic, shipping, and commercial arrangements; and through the International Labour Organization and the Health and Economic Committees of the League, more official backing and blessing were given to voluntary organizations. On the other hand, at the higher political and diplomatic levels, the 'new diplomacy' by international conference and the permanent machinery for consultation and collaboration at Geneva were fast breaking down without any overt reversion to the derided methods of the 'old diplomacy'. Nor, outside the American continent, were more limited regional groupings of like-minded states with common interests making their appearance. Open alliances were shunned as a reversion to the bad old ways, and inaction was justified by reliance upon the shattered machinery of the League. Aggressors and potential aggressors, in effect, were given an assurance that they could proceed with impunity. International statecraft in the nineteen-twenties, as applied to the crucial issue of preventing aggression, was as threadbare as the art of generalship had become during the first world war. The powers and cult of leadership lapsed to the new strong-arm dictatorships, all of whom happened to be opposed to the settlement and anxious

[1] S. H. Bailey: *The Framework of International Society* (1932), p. 29.

to destroy it. And meanwhile the more silent but no less menacing revolution of economic depression had come upon the world.

§3. *Economic Crisis*

The roots of the world economic crisis which began in 1929 lay more in the dislocation of international trade and of national economies by the world war than in the issues of war-debts and reparations payments, which were given so much attention during the nineteen-twenties. These bitterly disputed issues aggravated the economic aftermath of war because they diverted attention away from the more basic problems, and because both involved not a two-way traffic of goods, as in trade, but a one-way dumping of wealth from debtor to recipient.[1] During the war established trading contacts were broken, goods were produced not for export but for war-supplies, consumer-goods were sacrificed to war production, capital investments abroad were sold. By the end of the war world-markets had completely changed their character and location. New state frontiers usually meant new tariff barriers, especially in eastern Europe, and the great market of Russia was, for a time, isolated from the rest of the world's economy.

But at first, with the need to restore the damage and the production-lag of war and with the return of new resources of labour after demobilization, there was a burst of great prosperity. The boom of the early nineteen-twenties in each country accustomed people

[1] Both issues were virtually buried by the Lausanne Conference of 1932.

to the notion that peace and prosperity really did go
together. New commodities stimulated new popular
demands—for motor cars, radio sets, and films particularly: and in turn these prompted subsidiary demands,
for roads and garages, electrical equipment and cinemas. New developments, such as the mechanization of
agriculture, meant a demand for tractors. What was
almost a new phase of the industrial revolution accompanied post-war recovery, especially in the United
States and the western European countries.

The demand for such goods was made effective by
new systems of credit, including the hire-purchase
system which enabled consumers to enjoy these goods
before they could afford to pay for them. Internationally, too, schemes of reconstruction were launched on
loans. The world market rested, as before the war, on
complex mechanisms of international credit: and the
economic basis for the 'Locarno spirit' and the mood
of conciliation of the middle nineteen-twenties was the
temporary reconstitution of international credit. In this
process the issues of war-debts and reparations, so
controversial politically, played an important part. In
1921 the reparations payments demanded from Germany had been fixed at £6,600,000,000. The Dawes
Plan of 1924, which arranged for payments of this sum
to be made in annual instalments, also arranged for
Germany to receive a foreign loan of £40,000,000. This
loan was over-subscribed, more than half the total
coming from the United States and more than a
quarter from Great Britain. The success of the loan
was followed by an orgy of German borrowing, mainly

from the United States, and this influx of capital set up
a wave of prosperity. Few saw the dangers in the paradox of lending Germany money to pay back in reparations. Inter-allied war-debts became closely linked with
reparations, because France insisted that her payment
of debts depended on receipt of reparations. In all, they
amounted to nearly £4,000,000,000, with the United
States and Great Britain as the biggest creditor nations.
The repayment of these debts (except that of Russia,
which was repudiated by the Bolshevik government)
caused prolonged and complex international bickerings,
and again the vast transfers involved were made possible only by loans and credits from the United States.
The result was, therefore, a flow of short-term loans
across the Atlantic to Europe, creating a temporary
atmosphere of prosperity and well-being.

Partial payment of American debts in gold denuded
European states of it, at a time when gold was still the
ultimate basis of the international monetary system, as
well as of most national currencies. By the end of the
decade paper currencies began to depreciate in value.
The prosperity of Europe, and thereby of most of the
rest of the world, depended upon the willingness of
Americans to go on sending dollars across the Atlantic.
Should that suddenly cease, as it ceased in the autumn
of 1929, there were bound to be catastrophic consequences throughout the world. These consequences are
known as the world economic crisis.

Although experts still disagree about the precise
reasons for the crisis, it was undoubtedly connected
also with the depression in western agriculture which

brought wheat prices in the late nineteen-twenties to the lowest level in four hundred years. Because the more efficient agricultural methods of the western countries could produce more wheat than these countries could consume, and because the eastern countries of Asia which needed more wheat could not pay for it, it was the smaller countries exporting agricultural products which suffered first. Countries such as Argentina, Chile, Uruguay, Australia, and New Zealand found that, because their agricultural exports could not pay for their imports, more of their imports had to be paid for in gold. Slump began to follow boom. As the depression extended to other commodities, Britain too found that her gold reserves dwindled. By 1931 she went off the gold standard, and thereby devalued the pound sterling. More than twenty other countries, to defend their own industries against the competition of cheaper British goods, followed suit. Although most of the world's gold had gravitated to the United States, even she thought it prudent to abandon the gold standard for her currency. With this upheaval in the international monetary system, countries resorted to either governmental control of currency, or to simple barter, and in either case the smooth flow of international trade was further impeded. This contraction of the world market, combined with contraction of national income in the United States, spelt in human terms one major calamity: mass unemployment. By 1932 the United States had 15 million unemployed, Germany 6 million.

Unemployment, which had existed to some degree continuously after the war, and was in part due to the mechanization and 'rationalization' of industry, now increased with both the contraction of the world market and the economic crisis of 1931. It created a favourable climate for the new political movements of mass revolt which gained strength in the nineteen-thirties. Without mass purchasing power, mass production could not work: and with large-scale unemployment, purchasing power diminished. By 1932 there were 30 million persons unemployed in the world, in addition to many millions working short hours and more millions in Africa and Asia about whom there was no statistical knowledge. The immediate result was vast human suffering, personal frustration, social hardship: the ultimate result was that the victims turned, in desperation, to extremist political movements, of either communism or fascism, which promised to cure unemployment and provide a new basis for national recovery and material prosperity. Never were conditions in the western world more favourable to the ambitions of any demagogue or adventurer who had the insight and skill to exploit mass discontent. That is why in these years both communism and fascism became phenomena international in character, arising in one country after another on this rich soil of popular frustration and distress.

The world economic crisis burst with the collapse of the stock-exchange boom in New York in 1929. Wild and reckless speculation had driven the value of stocks and shares to fantastic heights. As soon as confidence was shaken a little, equally wild selling of stocks followed, which snowballed into a spectacular collapse of the stock market. Within one month stock values crashed by 40 per cent, and by 1932 5,000 American banks went bankrupt. Because Americans withdrew their investments from abroad, and bought less imports from abroad, the collapse quickly spread to other countries. Everywhere production slowed down, trade shrank, unemployment increased. In 1931 the main Viennese bank, the *Kredit-Anstalt*, failed, and this pre-cipitated the financial crisis in Europe. Between 1929 and 1932, world trade shrank to one third of its size, whilst the figures for unemployment grew.

In the face of such calamities governments and their expert advisers showed as little initiative and under-standing as they showed in their handling of inter-national diplomacy and politics. Things seemed, in every field, to have got out of hand. The obvious answer seemed to be a reassertion of control, which meant either a recourse to systematic economic plan-ning *à la Russe* or to dictatorial disciplining of national life *à l'Italien*. The United States, until the accession of President Roosevelt in 1933, preferred to trust to pri-vate initiative to produce order from the chaos. Her leaders mostly interpreted the crisis as an exceptionally acute form of the business cycle of boom and slump, and waited for the upturn of the cycle to lift America out of the depression. Britain in 1931 formed a National Government, given a so-called 'doctor's mandate' to tackle the problem as best they could. France, being more balanced and self-sufficient in her national econo-my and less sensitive to the fluctuations of international trade, suffered less early and less acutely than her neighbours. But in general governments were driven to manipulate and control currencies, and give some protection to their agriculture and industries. Economic nationalism, corresponding to the reversion to diplomatic separatism, dominated Europe. It was now each nation for itself. The United States passed the Hawley-Smoot tariffs in 1930, and in 1932 the British Commonwealth at the Ottawa Conferences adopted a system of imperial tariff preferences. The integrating forces of world economy had fallen apart as clearly as the international organization for preventing aggression had broken down. The years 1929–1931 were the lowest ebb since 1914 for general international co-operation.

4. Cultural Disintegration between the Wars

Along with these powerful disintegrating forces which disrupted the international system and the world economy there existed no less powerful forces inside each nation which corroded cultural unity and intellectual integrity, as well as social homogeneity. The nineteen-twenties were marked in Germany by a great social revolution which demolished her middle-class structure and by a moral decline which reduced her greatest cities to centres of vice; in the United States by all the social evils which accompanied the experiment in prohibition; in France by political scandals and a decline in public spirit; in Britain by disputes between capital and labour which culminated in the general strike of 1926; in India by recurrent riots and by the efforts of Mahatma Gandhi to expel the British from

I

his country and check industrialization; in European culture as a whole by exotic experiments in art and literature and neurotic adventures in artistic self-expression. None of the old order had been left unaffected by the earthquakes of war and the reverberations of economic depression. The methods of the gangster and the racketeer on one hand, the syndicalist strikers and fascist leagues on the other, were remarkably similar: and Marshal Goering, it was said, felt for his revolver when he heard the word 'culture'.

The divorce between the creative artist and his public, which had shown itself by 1914, now developed into a craze for coteries and esoteric experiences, of tortured efforts at self-expression appreciated by only a few and beyond the comprehension of the rest of mankind. In poetry, music, painting, and sculpture the smooth rhythms and lines of the established forms were regarded by the new generation of artists as unfitted to express the unrest and insecurity which, they felt prevailed in the post-war world. Free verse, dissonance, surrealism, seemed better adapted to express their vision of truth. Alike in painting and poetry, cubism led through 'dadaism' to surrealism, proclaiming on the way the 'absurdity of art' and 'the identity of contraries'. Dadaism, initiated by Tristan Tzara in Switzerland, was both a social and an artistic rebellion against all conventions. But it expressed in more extreme and anarchical form the same kind of impulse which produced the music of Stravinsky and Scriabin, the sculpture of Epstein, and the poetry of the Sitwells. In literature the vogue for D. H. Lawrence coincided with the growing interest in Freudian psychology and irrationalism; and James Joyce devoted sixteen years to producing a large work, *Finnegans Wake*, which most readers found quite incomprehensible. Occasionally a 'moderate modernist', like T. S. Eliot, could capture effectively the mood of the time in such poems as *The Waste Land* and *The Hollow Men* which a wider public could understand.

The chief features of cultural activity in Europe were a development of the inner conflicts already existing by 1914[1], now much exaggerated and complicated by the reactions against nationalism which followed the war. The revolt against intellectualism continued, enthroning the unconscious and feverishly experimenting with new styles, the more 'primitive' the better. The 'denationalization' of thought and art led to the abandoning of traditional values as well as conventional forms, and much was said of the need for *une littérature dégagée*. Along with the revolt against nationalism went a stronger sympathy for socialism and communism. This development became stronger in the nineteen-thirties, and the greatest French literary figure, André Gide, flirted with communism after 1933 until he actually visited Moscow in 1936. So the notion of *une littérature engagée* gradually gained force again. Auden and Spender succeeded to Virginia Woolf, Sartre to Cocteau. The stark and sordid realism of a Zola, which had seemed out of date in the 'twenties, returned in the form of the 'proletarian' novel, often written in the slang of the slums by 'men of the people', which meant

[1] See above, Chapter I, §3.

waiters, ex-burglars, and tramps. Soon after the war
'proletarian' opera had flourished in Germany, with
Kurt Weill's *Threepenny Opera* of 1928 and Alban
Berg's *Wozzeck* of 1922, although their audiences had
been unmistakeably bourgeois. Now, under the impulse
of the world economic slump, it revived with new vigour as dramatists and novelists discovered the tragedy
of mass unemployment and slum squalor. But they
were still out of touch with the wide public itself, which
had become increasingly avid for new forms of mass
entertainment requiring less intellectual effort. Popular
culture, impoverished by the divorce of artist from
public, could more easily become one of passive amuse-
ment, of mass sports, gambling, pulp magazines and
trashy writing, of jazz and jamborees.

Negative and depressing though the cultural history
of the inter-war years must be, it could show some
achievements of more permanent value wherever artistic effort chimed with the real needs and urges of
society. The ballet enjoyed great popularity and thrived
on it. In architecture men like Walter Gropius devised
new styles functionally adapted to modern construc-
tional materials and also well suited to the needs of
factories and schools in which members of a modern
urban community spend so much of their time. Some
of America's most beautiful skyscrapers and bridges
were built during these years, and evolved a style completely suited to their materials of steel and concrete.
As Nikolaus Pevsner has suggested, 'Nearly every
building that is designed nowadays serves masses and
not individuals. Must not therefore our style be one

adapted to mass production, in the sense of production not only in masses but also for masses?'[1] The London underground stations designed by Charles Holden were a strikingly successful example of such adaptation. Where innovation and experiment blended with more traditional values, as in the poetry of T. S. Eliot, the philosophy of Maritain and Berdyaev, the music of Vaughan Williams and Delius, artists of the time freed themselves from the merely transient mood. Their works are more likely to remain of lasting value when those of their more eccentric contemporaries will be of interest only to collectors of curious period pieces. Significant, too, is the international status of the Spanish-born philosopher, George Santayana, and of India's most talented and prolific literary man in modern times, Rabindranath Tagore. Spanning in their outlook and their appeal the continents of Asia, Europe, and America, both represent a real internationalism of culture.

Moreover, the consumption of culture in modern times has been very much greater than its production, and the cultural history of the inter-war years cannot be judged only in terms of its new writers and artists. The media for a much wider diffusion of culture were developed more than ever before. Wireless is the most powerful means ever invented for bringing music, literature, and ideas into the homes and everyday lives of ordinary families. The film, as a form of art, was developed during the inter-war years and cheap cinemas

[1] Nikolaus Pevsner: *An Outline of European Architecture* (1943), p. 265.

made it available to all. Easy and cheap means of travel widened the horizons of the middle classes. Cheap printing made good books purchasable by people of slight means, and public libraries made them available to all. Popular education was widened and improved as better supplies of trained teachers were built up. In eastern European, Asiatic, and African countries illiteracy began to be attacked with some vigour. In the Soviet Union and in Turkey the governments made intense efforts to raise the standards of literacy. In all these ways traditional culture was spread more widely among the masses than had seemed conceivable in 1919. But such facilities also afforded opportunities for national indoctrination and propaganda which few governments could resist and which the single-party states exploited to a remarkable degree. A 'nationalization' of popular culture took place *pari passu* with the tendencies towards 'denationalization' and cosmopolitanism in modern art: thus further widening the gulf between modern artists and their public.

American culture to a large extent enjoyed an immunity to these trends which was analogous to her policy of isolationism. This was partly because the philosophy of positivism and pragmatism held more unchallenged sway in the United States, where William James and John Dewey retained enormous influence; and social conditions in the nineteen-twenties corresponded to this outlook. It was an era of conformity and of general intolerance with non-conformity, despite the steady flow of social criticism maintained by a writer like Sinclair Lewis, and a certain welcome extended to poets of revolt. But the general assumptions of materialism reigned supreme, and the continued expansion of the country both in population and in wealth bred no radical challenge to the existing order, even to nationalism. As two distinguished American historians have put it,

Cities were bigger, buildings taller, roads longer, fortunes greater, automobiles faster, colleges larger, night clubs gayer, crimes more numerous, corporations more powerful, than ever before in history, and the soaring statistics gave to most Americans a sense of satisfaction if not of security.[1]

The collapse of 1929 came with all the greater a shock, and in the nineteen-thirties a greater heart-searching began.

Soviet culture, which by its novelties attracted so much attention and admiration abroad, was no less materialistic in tone. Nor was it, in the end, any less nationalistic, and although architecture, sculpture, and the drama enjoyed almost a renaissance under governmental encouragement, philosophy, the novel, and humane studies suffered more from the restrictions of Marxist orthodoxy than they gained in stimulus from the new and more eager public available for them.

The fascist régimes of Italy, Germany, and Spain showed from the start considerable hostility to modernism in art, which they regarded as a sign of decadence. They strove to reassert traditional national forms, but within the cramping and stultifying conditions laid

[1] A. Nevins and H. S. Commager: *America: The Story of a Free People* (1942), pp. 404–5.

down by the police state little creative activity in the arts was possible.[1]

Both the production and consumption of new ideas were greater in the sciences than in the arts. Here, at least, there was a close harmony of interest between the *élite* and the public. Characteristically, perhaps, the most popularized science was astronomy, and Sir James Jeans and Sir Arthur Eddington wrote best-sellers. But every western country evolved vastly greater facilities for scientific and technological education, and governments showered funds on scientific and industrial research. In Britain the Department of Scientific and Industrial Research was set up in 1916, and her example was soon followed by the Dominions and by France. By 1950 this important body had a parliamentary grant of £5,000,000 a year for financing research projects and maintaining a wide variety of research establishments. The first war in many respects promoted the growth of scientific knowledge of a utilitarian character. Medical facilities and medical knowledge were extended in most countries. The mathematical and physical sciences made spectacular progress. In 1919 Lord Rutherford succeeded in doing what medieval alchemists had failed to do: he broke through the barrier around the atomic kernel and transmuted nitrogen into oxygen. Under his guidance the nineteen-twenties became a golden age at the Cavendish

---

[1] One need only recall Herr Goebbels's famous 'book-burning', which condemned to the flames the works of such men as Einstein, Freud, Proust, and Wells, along with those of Marx, Gide, Upton Sinclair, and even Jack London, to assess the totalitarian conception of culture.

laboratory in Cambridge, and a brilliant team of re-
search-workers revealed the secrets of the atom and the
neutron; so unwittingly preparing the way for the invention of the atomic bomb.

Science, too, remained predominantly international
in character. During the nineteen-thirties it encountered increasing obstructions from the jealous single-
party states, but throughout the democratic countries
scientific knowledge accumulated and circulated fairly
freely. It was only after 1945 that scientists had reason
to become deeply worried by that conflict between
national obligations and demands and their duties to
mankind and to objective truth, which had so beset
artists and literary men two decades earlier. The schism
in world socialism, the fissures in nationalism, the
breakdown of internationalism, and the disruption of
the world economy were fittingly accompanied by the
splitting of even the atom. And that in turn, because of
its incalculable potentialities in a chaotic world, produced a certain nationalization of science.

Chapter Four
PRE-WAR DECADE, 1929–1939

§1. *Single-Party States*

THE essence of modern dictatorship is the monopoly of government by a political party which was forged, originally, to effect revolution. Lenin's achievement in leading the revolutionary Bolshevik Party to absolute power in Russia set the pattern for most subsequent revolutions: and paradoxically his most successful pupils were the leaders of anti-communist movements. Within five years of the Bolshevik Revolution Mussolini used his Fascist Party to establish a dictatorship in Italy, and two years after that Hitler, in *Mein Kampf*, outlined the possibilities of power before a similar German party which would be ruthless enough to overthrow the new Weimar Republic. Nor was the phenomenon of fascism peculiar to Italy and Germany. All the major European nations including Great Britain and France produced internal fascist movements of varying kinds during the nineteen-thirties independently of the Italian and German movements. The roots of fascism and of single-party dictatorship were European in character, and all the conditions necessary for their growth existed in the nineteen-twenties except the vital condition of acute economic distress among the middle classes. This the world economic crisis duly produced. That such distress did exist earlier, for special reasons, in Italy and Germany, explained the deeper roots of fascism in those two countries.

In a narrow sense, fascist movements represented a reaction of violent fear against the spread of communism. In Italy in 1922, in Germany in 1932, in Spain in 1936, they were in part strong-arm movements formed among ex-servicemen or military groups to fight the growth of communism. They drew support from all who feared an attack on private property and capitalism, and they particularly exploited nationalist grievances. They reduced complex issues to the crudest terms— Germany had not been defeated but had been stabbed in the back, Italy had won the war but lost the peace, and in each case it was the fault of the liberals, socialists, and pacifists. They thus combined a wide popular demagogic appeal with special appeals to group interests and fears.

But in a wider sense they were an outcrop of the nineteenth-century spread of universal suffrage, of a mass civilization. They operated on the principle that a modern revolution can best be achieved (and can perhaps, in advanced nations, only be achieved) by a party which is already in power. They therefore concentrated on attaining power as far as possible by constitutional means, and to do this they had to make a mass appeal to the most easily aroused emotions of the populace. Learning something from the methods of democratic parties and even more from those of commercial advertisers, they rode to power on stimulated waves of fear and anger, hatred and envy. They elaborated the techniques of the mass-meeting and the parade. They denied in action that man is a reasonable and thinking creature; a denial which twentieth-century psychologists and philosophers had already made in print. National Socialists were urged to 'think with their blood', and Hitlerism was anti-semitic mainly because racial prejudice was the quickest way to destroy rational modes of thought. Again, because democracy still had some mass appeal, fascists were careful to pay it considerable homage through terrorized elections, packed parliaments, and bogus plebiscites, even whilst they denounced it in theory. Mussolini and Hitler each came from a lowly family, each attained the rank of non-commissioned officer in the war, and each posed as a man of the people.

Mussolini had been a socialist in his earlier years, and the original *Deutsche Arbeiterpartei* included some socialists. Both movements included some socialistic objectives in their programmes even whilst they denounced democratic socialism. The corporative state was presented as an enlightened method of settling disputes between capital and labour, and the National Socialist Twenty-Five Points of 1923 talked much of 'ending the thraldom of interest'. Each demanded (and here they were more sincere) a strong state to control the whole national economy in the interests of the nation: but they identified party with nation, and the strength of the state was to come from the personal leadership of the party.

Having exploited every difficulty of the parliamentary governments and every popular grievance, the parties succeeded—amid some show of violence—in gaining power with constitutional formalities. The real fascist revolutions followed, and like the Bolshevik Revolution were carried out by a party which already controlled all the power mechanisms of the state. Police and army were reinforced by secret police and party militias, and were used to crush every form of opposition. A reign of terror was instituted whilst the party consolidated its grip. And the party, having served so well as the agency for effecting revolution, was preserved (after due purging) as the instrument of the new tyranny. Disciplined, centralized, indoctrinated, privileged, it occupied all the key positions in the state and in national life. Thus it became possible to have not only absolute power but totalitarian power, for no limits were admitted to the scope of state competence. Churches were reduced to political impotence, free trade unions destroyed and strikes forbidden, free associations demolished or absorbed. Every agency for moulding public opinion—the schools, the press, radio, cinema, public meetings—was taken under party control. No element of social life was accepted as lying beyond the direction of the government. Never before in the history of the world had ruthless men enjoyed such complete and far-reaching power over the lives of millions. Former dictators, if equally absolute, had not been equally totalitarian in their aims. The fascist dictators combined the hysterical mass appeal of a Robespierre with the powerful governmental machinery of a Napoleon, and added to both the whole repertoire of devices which tend to increase the power of any modern government: the machine-gun, scientific taxation, an efficient civil service.

Within a decade of the apparent triumph of liberal

democracy in the world, Europe and Asia were confronted with the most complete denials of democratic ideals and institutions. By a remarkable paradox a civilization which had rested on respect for individual personality, for objective truth gained by the free quest of the spirit and by free clash of argument, had bred within itself movements which denied its very fundamentals. When the relation both of the world war and of the economic crisis to this development has been fully explained, the explanation still seems to fall short. Fascism, and in many respects communism too, would seem to have a deep appeal in certain conditions to the 'little man' of modern civilization. Hitler suggested the connexion when he wrote, in *Mein Kampf*, that 'Mass demonstrations must burn into the little man's soul the proud conviction that though a little worm he is nevertheless part of a great dragon'. Could there be any better account of the meaning of aggressive nationalism?

.   .   .   .   .

The natural affinities of the fascist régimes and their hope of mutual gain by 'pooling their nuisance-values' led in 1936 to the so-called Rome-Berlin Axis and to joint intervention in the Spanish Civil War on the side of the rebels against the Spanish Republican government. This intervention, accompanied by the non-intervention of the western powers, helped to ensure the triumph of the rebels, led by General Franco, in 1939. The régime Franco then set up owed much to the model of fascist Italy. In 1936, too, a third partner was brought into the alliance. The Japanese régime had

certain affinities with the fascists, and above all it shared
a common enmity towards the United States, Great
Britain, and the western European powers, and was in
quest of economic and territorial gains at their expense.
Japan, like Germany, had left the League of Nations in
1933. She had no immediate conflict of interests with
Germany or Italy, and her experience of western weakness in face of her Manchurian aggression encouraged
her to defy the western powers again. Since the immediate and professed enemy was communism, she signed
with Germany an 'Anti-Comintern Pact', ostensibly
aimed against the spread of communism. A year later
(in 1937) Italy adhered to it.

The basic division between the single-party states on
one hand (amongst which Japan may be included) and
the multi-party states on the other, was until 1939
blurred by a triangular pattern of conflicts of national
interests in the world. In the west were the two maritime and colonial powers of Britain and France, opposed to the revision of the peace settlement but not in
accord about foreign policy except for a short period
after 1924; and associated with them were the smaller
states of western and eastern Europe, the Dominions
of the British Commonwealth, and more loosely still
the United States. In central Europe were Germany
and Italy, and in the Far East was Japan, each for its
own nationalist reasons a revisionist power, hostile to
the League and determined upon territorial expansion.
Straddling Europe and Asia was the Soviet Union, increasingly active in European affairs since her entry into
the League in 1934, but basically hostile to both the

other groups. Relations between any two of these three groups inevitably affected the third. Any drawing together of the first two, as at Locarno in 1925 or Munich in 1938, looked like an anti-Soviet bloc. Any *rapprochement* between the western states and the Soviet Union, as when Russia joined the League or as in the Spanish Civil War, meant encirclement for Germany and even Italy and seemed to bring the tide of communism closer to Europe. Any sign of German-Soviet liaison, as at Rapallo in 1922 or in the Nazi-Soviet Pact of 1939, revealed the cleavage between the single-party states and the multi-party democracies. Just as before 1914, the system of *rapprochements*, *ententes* and alliances brought constant fear and uncertainty in international relations; only now it was a more complex and shifting system of alliances instead of the relatively clear-cut dichotomy of 1914.

These conflicting national interests and the shifts of *rapprochement* dictated by them were overlaid by a triangle of social and ideological conflicts. By the decade of the nineteen-thirties, each of the three groups of states had come to be identified with a particular form of political, social, and economic régime, and even with a particular ideology or *Weltanschauung*. But these differences of social structure and ideological outlook were not sharply defined, and the systems overlapped. Any two of them could be regarded as having elements in common. Thus there arose 'ideological fronts' which were usually negative in form: the anti-Comintern Pact for the 'defence of European civilization against Bolshevism'; the anti-Fascist coalition and Popular Front governments of 1935–1937; the Nazi-Soviet Pact

of 1939 and the partition of Poland between Germany
and the Soviet Union. Each was a tune played according to the affinities and opportunities of the moment.
By the end of 1941 it seemed that these criss-cross
patterns had clarified into a simple and firm design.
Germany's attack on the Soviet Union forced a firm
alliance between Russia and the west, and Japan's
attack on Pearl Harbour led Germany and Italy to de-
clare war on the United States and forced on America
an active alliance with both the Soviet Union and the
western European powers. But by 1946 this clarity had
again dispersed, and the old fundamental cleavage between the single-party states of the Soviet bloc and
the multi-party democracies emerged in all its
starkness.

In truth, to regard the international tensions and
conflicts of the inter-war years as essentially ideological
conflicts was as much an over-simplification as to regard them as purely conflicts of national interests.
Divisions between nations were an amalgam of both,
and the ideological split penetrated inside each nation
as well as into relations between states. Hence it was
that most countries produced both communist and
fascist movements on their own soil, and conquest
usually took the form of exploiting domestic differences
and supporting quisling or puppet governments. In so
far as the world had been made one, conflicts of interest
and outlook transcended national frontiers: in so far as
the world was still divided into distinct national states
and territorial communities, differences of interest and
outlook fell along national boundaries. The complex

K

nature of inter-war alignments and of war-time up
heavals sprang ultimately from the stage of semi
unification in which the world had been left by the
developments of the years before 1914.[1]

Moreover, in even the multi-party states, govern
ments were increasingly expected, and in varying de
grees were increasingly compelled, to undertake mor
active responsibilities for the security and welfare o
their peoples. The tendency for governments to become
more powerful and more multifarious in their activities
was world-wide. Parliamentary systems had to adjus
themselves to the need for stronger and more drasti
executive action. In Britain this took the form of a
national coalition in 1931, although the bulk of the
Labour Party did not follow its leaders into the coali
tion. In France it took the form of more frequent grants
of emergency powers, whereby governments could
issue decree-laws to meet the economic crisis; and in
1936 the Popular Front, an unusually wide left-wing
coalition, attempted to catch up on overdue social
legislation. In the United States there occurred the
most sensational development of all in the New Deal o
Franklin D. Roosevelt in 1933. In effect, it meant the
extension of federal authority and especially of Presi
dential power to counter the effects of the economi
crisis on national finance, mass unemployment, and
industrial dislocation. Thus one of the President's
earliest and less sensational measures, the Glass
Steagall Act of June 1933 was designed to restore con
fidence in American banking. In effect it opened new

[1] See above, Chapter I, §2.

avenues of state control. In Professor Denis Brogan's words, the Act, 'together with the control over the dollar given to President Roosevelt, ended the old autonomy of the American credit structure, and, almost unnoticed, began an extraordinary extension of the directing and regulating powers of the Treasury Department.'[1]

Other countries adjusted themselves to the economic blizzard in other ways. For some it meant the end of an unstable parliamentary system. In Austria, the European country where the economic crisis had first produced catastrophic effects, the Chancellor Dollfuss destroyed the democratic republic, suppressed the Socialist Party, and governed by emergency decrees until he was assassinated by the Nazis in 1934. In Poland, where parliamentary government had worked increasingly badly under the constitution of 1921, Marshal Pilsudski wielded almost autocratic power after his military *coup d'état* of 1930; and in 1935, when he died, a new constitution and new franchise laws gave power to a group led by his former 'Colonels'. In 1934 a similar military *coup d'état* overthrew the unsatisfactory parliamentary system in Bulgaria, and the next year King Boris assumed a royal dictatorship. By the end of the nineteen-thirties every one of the Balkan states had become a dictatorship of some kind. Similar tendencies showed themselves in countries as far away as South America. In 1933 President Terra of Uruguay, on the plea that the world economic depression and its effects on the country called for prompt and decisive

[1] D. W. Brogan: *Roosevelt and the New Deal* (1952), p. 36.

action, staged a *coup d'état* and prepared a new constitution. In Mexico the revolution which had begun in 1910 entered a new phase in 1934 with the Presidency of Càrdenas, whose six-year plan of land distribution and nationalization had effects not incomparable with those of the Soviet Five-Year Plans. For other countries where constitutional parliamentary government sprang from deeper and firmer roots, it meant new efforts to produce broad-based coalitions of national unity, parallel to the National Government in Britain or the Doumergue National Union government in France. Thus Belgium, whose dependence upon foreign trade made her economy particularly sensitive to the depression, in 1935 formed an all-party government under Paul van Zeeland. His Belgian New Deal, based on devaluation and structural reforms of the fiscal and banking systems, met with violent opposition from a combination of Flemish nationalists and Rexists, and the latter won twenty-one seats in the Belgian Chamber in 1936.[1] In the Union of South Africa the Nationalist party, led by Hertzog, was forced by the economic depression into combination with the South African party led by Smuts, which inaugurated a new phase of national government after 1934. The same year brought a coalition government in Australia.

[1] The rise of Rexism in Belgium is almost a microcosm of the rise of fascist movements elsewhere. The party was founded in 1934 by Léon Degrelle who showed a flair for appealing to a combination of violent nationalism, conservative Catholicism, the sentiments of the army-officer class, big industrialists, middle classes who had suffered from devaluation, and the unemployed. It was well on the way to decline by 1939, but its survivors served as German puppets after 1940.

General features of such adjustments in the democratic countries were the stubborn opposition which greater governmental activity encountered, and the half-heartedness of many of the governmental measures. In Britain the National Government was slow and reluctant to adopt measures of large-scale public works, the only serious remedy proposed for mass unemployment. In France the Popular Front government of M. Léon Blum was refused emergency powers by the conservative Senate. In the United States President Roosevelt met with severe resistance, first from the Supreme Court and then from the Republican Party, still wedded to the doctrines of Presidents Hoover and Coolidge in the nineteen-twenties that the natural working of the business cycle would lift the country out of the depression. The political tensions in each country generated by the conflict between communist and fascist movements threatened public order, and much of the energy which governments should have been expending on promoting economic recovery and providing greater social security had to be spent on stopping the rival extremists from rending the country in two and destroying public peace. Everywhere democrats were faced with the problem of how far they could afford to tolerate the intolerant. Both communists and fascists claimed on democratic principles the freedom of speech and demonstration which they were committed to destroy once they should gain power themselves. Yet democrats, fearful lest by suppressing these movements they might themselves destroy the civil rights and liberties which they cherished, suffered from paralysis of decision and action. In the countries bordering on Germany this same problem was made even more acute by the existence of the considerable national minority groups left by the Versailles settlement. German minorities in Czechoslovakia and Poland, and fascist groups in Austria, were increasingly used as activist groups to disrupt the régimes in preparation for Hitlerite conquests. Here, too, the conflict between democratic régimes committed to seeking government by a majority and single-party régimes committed to establishing government by a minority emerged as the basic political issue in Europe.

§2. *The Fusion of Nationalism and Socialism*

Bolshevism and fascism were alike, in one aspect, apotheoses of the nation state. In another aspect they were alike denials of its validity. When Lenin succeeded in organizing Bolshevik power on a national scale in Russia, and Stalin launched the Five Year Plans for the economic development and modernization of the Soviet Union, they found themselves committed to the experiment of establishing communism in a single country. The triumph of Stalin over Trotsky, completed by the purges of 1935 and the new 'liberal' constitution of 1936, marked the climax of this process. The Bolsheviks had discovered that they could save communism only by nationalizing it. Similarly, the fascist movements found that they could enlist the sympathies and interests of the majorities of their peoples only by undertaking to give protection against the social insecurities of the economic crisis. They favoured policies of autarky and social reorganization. If this process, by which governing parties perpetuate and consolidate their power by providing what their peoples most need in conditions of economic crisis and depression, may be labelled a process of 'socialization', then it may be said that they too found that they could save nationalism only by socializing it. Similarly, in the multi-party states, the demand made of all governments, in the nineteen-thirties, was for a more vigorous and effective pursuit of the ends of social security and human welfare. The way had been paved for these demands by the growth of universal suffrage before 1914. Everywhere it had been accompanied by the provision of popular education, factory legislation, provision for public health, old-age pensions, and the rest. In conditions of economic depression the need for a rapid extension of such protection seemed plain. And the gradual penetration, even beyond communist and socialist movements, of Marxist ideas and of faith in the capacity of governments to perform those impressive feats of social organization which they had accomplished during the first world war, made such a demand now irresistible. In face of the nationally disruptive forces of communism and fascism, as well as of the socially disintegrating forces of economic depression, it seemed that in the democracies, too, nationalism could be saved only by socializing it.

For these reasons the most striking feature of world history during this decade is the interpenetration of the ideas of nationalism and socialism. Everywhere that mattered the state was becoming not only stronger in

power, and not only more totalitarian in its competence:
it was also becoming more socialistic in its aims. Moreover, states remained strong in proportion as they
showed their effectiveness for fulfilling the purposes of
social security and human welfare. In France the state
lost the confidence of the people so far as it showed itself
reluctant or ill-suited to carry through timely social
reforms. Britain, already enjoying the long traditions of
liberal social reform and Fabian socialism, remained
strong in spite of the paucity of firm measures to cure
unemployment and save families from destitution: and
the much-maligned dole, or system of unemployment
relief, undoubtedly did much to save her from greater
social unrest. In the United States the 'New Deal' was
condemned as being back-door socialism when its
leaders were not being attacked as neo-fascists. The
highly individualist traditions of America resisted the
new extent of federal activity in organizing agricultural
and industrial pump-priming, civilian conservation
corps and a Tennessee Valley Authority. But even there,
where great natural resources and wealth and a high
standard of living softened the blow of economic crisis,
national recovery involved a certain infusion of socialism.

It was thus no accident that the Hitlerite movement
in Germany clung to its title of National Socialism, and
made much of its efforts to relieve unemployment by
schemes of public works and rearmament. The main-
spring of the demand for socialism was the discovery
that Germans made during the currency crash of 1923,
and most other peoples made during the economic
crisis, that the individual or the family is helpless in the

face of economic slump. It was traditional, in such depressions, for governments to undertake some measures
of relief. Elizabethan England and France of the *ancien
régime* had done so. But there were three novelties in
the situation at this time. One was the severity and
world-wide nature of the economic crisis. The second
was the greater faith in the efficacy of governmental
action induced by the war and by the growth of socialistic ideas. The third was the need for any governing
party to enlist the interest and support of a majority of
the people if, in twentieth-century conditions, it were
to hold on to power at all. The manner in which
nationalism and socialism fused depended, therefore,
on the variations from country to country in the
potency of these three new factors.

The Soviet Union, committed to a vast programme
of communization, needed to enlist the forces of Russian nationalism if it were to survive in a world of capitalist powers. Although its planned economy enabled
the Stalinist government to shelter the country from
the worst ravages of the economic blizzard, Russian
trade with the rest of the world was deeply affected by
the world slump in prices and Stalin felt it necessary to
purge from the party Trotskyites and any other forces
resisting complete concentration on the establishment
of communism in a single country. The effect was to
make Russian communism more exclusively nationalistic. Germany, committed to an intensely nationalistic
programme of reuniting all Germans into the Third
Reich and of shaking off all relics of international control, needed to destroy all forces within the party which

sought to promote a 'second revolution' and to press demands for more extensive social reforms than were immediately necessary. Thus, as in Russia, the years 1934–1935 brought a savage purge of the party. In the 'Night of the Long Knives' (30 June 1934) Hitler rid himself of his embarrassing 'second revolutionaries', the German counterpart to Trotskyites.

One consequence of these events was that socialism lost most of its former internationalist flavour, and became even more sharply distinguished from communism. The split that had appeared at Zimmerwald in 1915 became permanent. Even in the Popular Front government in France, the Communist Party whilst supporting the Socialists would not participate in the ministries. It had originally been chronological circumstance rather than logical affinities which made socialism internationalist in outlook. In the nineteenth century socialism had been internationalist mainly because liberalism was internationalist: but its emphasis upon the power of the state to effect reforms meant that, in an era of nation states, it was bound in time to become more nationalistic. The Second International had foundered on this very rock, and even the Communist International operated only in so far as the Russian Communist Party activated and dominated it. Parliamentary socialist movements, renouncing revolutionary action, inevitably became more nationalist in character. The workers of the world showed themselves both unwilling and unable to unite.

Meanwhile the restless fascist dictators sought to stimulate nationalistic sentiments by other means. They

mbarked on foreign aggressions, claiming always that
hey were merely asserting a natural national right
itherto denied them. As early as 1923 Mussolini had
ullied Greece and spurned the League over Corfu.
ut until 1934 he had followed a foreign policy which
erved Italy's national interests. He had saved the
alkans from a German influence which would have
usted Italy from her natural economic hinterland
vhen he prevented an *Anschluss* between Austria and
Germany. When the Austrian Nazis murdered Chan-
ellor Dollfuss in 1934, Mussolini massed Italian troops
n the Brenner Pass as a warning to Hitler that he
ould not then annex Austria: and Hitler, being un-
eady for war, accepted the warning. But from 1935 on-
vards the Duce embarked on an imperialistic campaign
o capture Abyssinia, to claim Tunisia, Nice, and Savoy
rom France, and make the Mediterranean an 'Italian
Lake'. Italian participation in the Spanish Civil War
vas prompted by similar considerations. Italy's pre-
ccupation southwards, especially when the League of
Nations was galvanized into applying economic sanc-
ions against her, gave Hitler the opportunity to occupy
nd remilitarize the Rhineland in March 1936 and to
ffect the *Anschluss* with Austria by 1938. In that year
e also began a campaign against Czechoslovakia which
ulminated in the disruption of that multi-national
lemocratic state by the Munich agreement and total
German occupation of the country in March 1939.
These expansionist moves by the two dictators, and the
elative ineffectiveness of British and French resistance to
hem, rallied nationalist sentiments at home behind the

dictators. Popularity came with success, and aggrieve
nationalist sentiment came with foreign resistance.

It was not only in Europe and the United States tha
the forces of nationalism and socialism were allie
Throughout the whole colonial world, powerful move
ments demanding a greater measure of independenc
and self-government were gaining voice and strength
In China the Communist Party was rivalling th
nationalist Kuomintang as the popular movement for
national resistance to Japan which would also secur
more drastic social overhaul. In India a socialist lik
Jawaharlal Nehru was coming forward as a more mili
tant champion of independence than the pacifis
Mahatma Gandhi, although he still remained the sup
porter and ally of the man whom Hindus had come t
regard as a saviour. The main difference between them
—and it was important—was that whereas Gandhi re
sisted westernization and industrialism, Nehru and hi
supporters would accept industrialism and use it t
increase Indian standards of living. They were agree
on the need to shake off British rule first. In all Asi
the example and influence of the Soviet Union wer
great. Throughout the whole colonial world, in Afric
in Indonesia, in Indo-China, the ideas and ideals
social welfare were following fast on the heels of indus
trialism and imperialism. They flowed into the move
ments for national independence, and prepared for tha
great colonial revolution which was released by th
second world war.[1]

* * * * *

[1] Cf. below, Chapter VI, §3.

In the whole process of fusion and confusion between the tendencies making for nationalism and the tendencies making for socialism, there is no question of one being the horse and the other the cart. It is truer to regard both as simply different aspects of one larger trend to which many different factors and events contributed. These factors included the simultaneous strengthening of both nationalism and socialism by the necessities of warfare between 1914 and 1918; the instinctive reaction of men and of nations to the world economic crisis; the widespread popular demand for higher standards of living and for greater social and economic security, which parties seeking to keep or gain power attempted to satisfy; and even basic economic developments, such as the spread of industrialization to a larger area of the earth combined with increasing barriers to migration, and the new possibilities of production opened up by scientific and technological discoveries.

Since it has so often been argued that nationalism is an anomaly or anachronism in the face of the global interdependence produced by world trade and the progress of science, it is important to recall that even the discoveries of science may weaken interdependence and revivify nationalism. The discovery, partly by German scientists during the British blockade of Germany, of cheap ways to make nitrates for fertilizer from the air instead of importing them from overseas, largely demolished the flourishing trade with South America. Henceforth Europe, if it so wished, could be self-contained for nitrate fertilizer. The invention of neon lighting to replace filaments made from tungsten or

other rare metals; of plastics capable of replacing wood
or metal or textiles; of artificial rubber and similar
ersatz substances; of detergents which, by releasing the
supplies of fats otherwise needed for soap, can suddenly
increase the world's supply of margarine: these, and
many similar developments, are at least as conducive to
greater national independence in economic life as to
greater world interdependence. What may be bad for
world trade may be good for national production, and
may actually increase national productivity and standards of living. The best way to get something is not
always to transport it from the farthest corners of the
earth where it happens to be in natural supply, even
though modern transport has made this so easy. Similarly, throughout the period since 1914, the development of hydro-electric power made some nations much
less dependent on overseas supplies of petroleum or
coal than they had been hitherto: and industrial appli-
cations of atomic energy may effect an even more drastic revolution in the extent to which one nation must
rely on another for its resources of basic power. Such
developments, indeed, are almost as much an explanation of the modern tendencies towards nationalism and
more powerful state organizations as they are consequences of these tendencies. As more areas of the earth
develop industries of their own, the old division between industrial nations and those areas from which
they draw their supplies of raw materials and their cus-
tomers inevitably gets blurred: and it becomes increasingly tempting for each nation to try to build up a
more balanced and self-sufficient economy.

In economic terms, this process meant that economic nationalism was not merely a reactionary effort to escape from the competition of other countries or a revived mercantilism chiefly concerned with national power and security. Political and normal protectionist considerations certainly played their part in the revival of economic nationalism during the inter-war years. Industries which grew up like mushrooms during the war were readily given protection after the war; and labour organizations were never slow to seek all kinds of safeguards against competition from cheaper foreign labour. But one important and constant factor was that economic self-sufficiency had become more practically possible, and the old organic interdependence of the continents, which had involved European superiority and privilege, had been broken by the war and its commercial consequences. As in political developments so in economic, the German cult of totalitarian dictatorship and the German drive for autarky were expressions of world tendencies carried to their most extreme phase. And the economic consequences of the war were even more far-reaching and momentous than the economic consequences of the peace about which Lord Keynes wrote so eloquently.

In political terms this process means that democratic ideals, too, carried within themselves a drive towards the creation of a strong and more positive state. The connexion between democratic ideas and institutions and the concepts of *laissez-faire*, so apparent in the history of Great Britain and the United States, was largely due to historical and therefore to temporary circumstances. In France and in many other European countries, democracy has always had more totalitarian and more socialistic associations.[1] Even the utilitarian slogan, 'the greatest happiness of the greatest number', had no essential connexions with individualism in economics and *laissez-faire* in politics, though it had with political equality. It was in essence a statement of social purpose which its advocates are in no way logically precluded from pursuing by socialistic means. Once 'the greatest happiness of the greatest number' is believed to lie in the systematic provision of greater social security, as well as in equal political and civil rights, then the utilitarian state becomes a positive and socialistic state.

Nor is that form of political organization most closely identified with national consciousness and unity obviously an unsuitable agency to perform such functions. If it is intelligent it will co-operate, as far as it can, with other nation-states to achieve those parts of its tasks which call for international co-operation: but there are many parts of its task which it can well fulfil, and which no other agency could fulfil so well.

Finally, it may not be fanciful to detect in this universal alliance and merger between the forces of nationalism and of socialism a certain uneasy awareness that the appeal of nationalism needed to be reinforced by the appeal of socialism. If the enlightened despotisms of the later eighteenth century in Europe earned

[1] See the admirable study of such tendencies by J. Talmon: *The Origins of Totalitarian Democracy* (1952).

or that era the label of 'an age of repentant monarchy', may not the socialized nationalism of the mid-twentieth century come to be regarded as a sign of repentant nationalism? It was as if the original impulses and attractions of nationalism and patriotism, overworked and partially discredited by the world wars, sought new strength and moral justification in promoting and serving the ideals of social welfare. The ideal of equality began to exert stronger attractions than the ideal of liberty, the claims of society became no less insistent than the claims of the nation-state.[1] If so, this was some reason for optimism: because it meant that nationalism was becoming, in the minds of men, less an end in itself than a means to other ends. And, provided that democratic methods could prevail over those of totalitarian absolutism, the state might at last be used to serve the needs of man rather than making man exist for the state.

3. International Co-operation

The extent of international co-operation during the pre-war decade is misjudged if the failure of the League of Nations to provide security against aggression and to achieve a peaceful settlement of international disputes is alone considered. Not only did a wide area of general co-operation in technical matters, such as the activities of the Health Committee and of the International Labour Organization, survive the disruptions of the dictators and the weakness of will of the democracies:

---

[1] For elaboration of this idea, see the present writer's study of *Equality* (1949).

L

but two other important agencies of co-operation amongst nations gained in solidarity and strength during these years. They were the Pan American organizations and the British Commonwealth of Nations: and even as arrangements for mutual defence and collective security, both proved to be very much more effective than the League when the acid test of war was applied after 1939.

The chief landmarks in the growth of Pan American co-operation were the Havana Conference of 1928, President Roosevelt's 'Good Neighbour' policy proclaimed in 1933, the Inter-American Conference for the Maintenance of Peace at Buenos Aires in 1936, and the eighth Pan American Conference held at Lima in 1939. The United States progressively gave up its former claim to intervene in the affairs of the smaller Caribbean states, made a series of eleven reciprocal trade agreements with the Latin-American countries, and led the movement for collective consultation in the event of any threat to the peace of the continent from within or without. By 1939, as a result of these policies, 'far closer and more genuinely co-operative relations had been established between the American republics than at any time in their history', and 'the contrast now was not between the bright hopes of the League of Nations and the halting progress of the Pan American movement, but between the failing vitality of the League and a Pan American movement infused with new vigour.'[1]

[1] R. A. Humphreys: *The Evolution of Modern Latin America* (1946), p. 154.

The course of British Commonwealth development in these years was towards a loosening of the formal bonds and recognition of the complete autonomy of each Dominion over its own commercial and foreign policy. The Statute of Westminster, passed in 1931, marked the culmination of the century-long process towards Dominion self-government and self-determination. The Ottawa Conference of 1932 revealed that economic planning on a Commonwealth scale was ruled out, that the commercial relations of the Dominions cut across their imperial connexions, and that they were all highly protectionist in outlook. The main reason was that they had, since 1914, developed industries of their own and were no longer primarily producers of food and raw materials for the British market. The most that could be achieved at Ottawa was a general agreement to keep protective duties at a level which would give British producers 'full opportunity of reasonable competition'. In these ways, whilst the trend of Pan American relations was in the direction of closer co-operation, that of Commonwealth relations seemed to be towards greater separatism. Yet when the British government declared war on Germany in 1939 its example was followed immediately by Australia and New Zealand, and within a week by Canada and the Union of South Africa. Eire alone remained neutral. At no time during the long war was there any risk of a Dominion withdrawing from the war, and the non-self-governing colonies showed equal loyalty and solidarity. Their collective contributions to the war were enormous, and under the test of concerted action in war the

Commonwealth proved even stronger than the Pan American group.[1]

It is in relation to the comparative success of these two modes of international co-operation that the record of the League of Nations as a medium of co-operation must be considered. It may be argued that the decline of the League helped to accelerate the growth of Pan American organizations,[2] just as it can be argued that British efforts to reconcile the commercial interests of the Commonwealth helped to aggravate the effects of the economic depression for other countries.[3] Certainly there was never close co-operation between the League and the Pan American Union (largely because of the absence of the United States from the League); and the Latin American states which had all previously been members of the League tended to withdraw from it during the nineteen-thirties and to seek greater security in Pan Americanism. There were some advantages in having a variety of different forms and media of international co-operation, and it was too often assumed by enthusiastic internationalists that unless organizations were universal or potentially universal in scope they were worthless. Co-operation, like peace,

[1] When the United States entered the war in December 1941 the six Central American and the three island republics immediately followed suit. Mexico and Brazil entered the war in 1942, Bolivia and Colombia in 1943; but Argentina, Chile, Ecuador, Paraguay, Peru, Venezuela, and Uruguay did not enter until 1945.

[2] Cf. R. A. Humphreys, *op. cit.*, pp. 154–5.

[3] The Ottawa agreements of 1932 certainly encouraged high tariffs against imports from countries outside the Commonwealth and were bitterly criticized for this by European countries.

may have many palaces. Neither the Pan American
Union nor the Commonwealth was completely successful in reconciling the national interests of its members.
Bolivia and Paraguay were at war between 1933 and
1935, and as late as 1941 Peru and Ecuador resorted to
arms against one another. The hostilities between India
and Pakistan about Kashmir, like the tensions within
the Union of South Africa, have been serious blemishes
in the record of the Commonwealth. But at least
throughout the nineteen-thirties both were notably
stronger and more cohesive units than the more comprehensive organization of the League.

The reasons for this are complex, but they cannot be
sought mainly in the realm of economic interests. The
links of trade between the Latin American countries
have always been weaker than their trading connexions
with either the United States or Great Britain. By 1938
trade between the Latin American countries was less
than one-tenth of the total trade of the area, and three-
fifths of their whole exports went outside the hemis-
phere—mainly to Britain and Europe. Likewise, some
three-fifths of Great Britain's exports went to countries
outside the Commonwealth, and it remains very debatable whether even the Ottawa agreements did succeed in increasing the total amount of trade within the
Commonwealth. It seems likely that within both groups
of nations the chief forces of cohesion were on the one
hand certain common traditions and cultural forces,
and on the other the greater certainty that members
of the group would in fact treat an attack upon one as
an attack upon all. Throughout the inter-war years it

was always more certain that aggression by a major external power upon either a member of the Pan American Union or upon a part of the British Commonwealth would lead to a rallying of forces on the part of the other members, than it was ever certain that aggression against a member of the League would lead to concerted action by the other members of the League.

The ineffectiveness of the League of Nations to prevent or to check Japanese aggression against China was the first serious blow to its prestige as an agency for providing security. But a rapid succession of other demonstrations quickly followed: Italy's attack upon Abyssinia in 1935, Germany's absorption of Austria in March, 1938, her triumph against Czechoslovakia at Munich in September 1938 and her annexation of the rest of that country in March 1939; Italy's occupation of Albania in April 1939. These demonstrations that the sanctions Articles of the Covenant were valueless as guarantees of collective action against aggression were given *pari passu* with demolition of the articles in the Treaty of Versailles which had been designed to restrain Germany: particularly the remilitarization of the Rhineland in 1936 and the blatant rearmament of Germany, which violated Articles 42–44 and the whole of Part V of the Treaty. German invasion of Austria and Czechoslovakia also violated Articles 80–81. Not only was the Treaty of Versailles demolished, but several subsequent treaties were equally violently broken. This was important, since it came to be generally believed that many stipulations of the Treaty of Versailles had

been originally unreasonable and should by now have
been revised, and that the *Diktat* of 1919 left Germany
without clear moral obligation to respect its terms. But
no such plea could be made when Germany broke the
treaties of Locarno which she had signed voluntarily,
the Kellogg Pact of 1928, and even the Nazi Treaty with
Poland of 1934. The collapse of the League brought
with it total loss of faith in the sanctity of all treaties.
It shattered confidence in the value of any international
agreement, however solemn. It is significant that the
most solid alliance between nations in 1939 was that
which rested on no formal agreements whatever—the
British Commonwealth.

The main feature of internationalism between the
two wars was not, therefore, a break-down of machinery or lack of adequate organization:[1] it was a
failure of will to implement the principles which had
been adopted in 1919. Since this failure might be due
either to a lack of will on the part of the members of the
League or to the fact that the principles were themselves incapable of implementation in the conditions of

[1] The great diversity and complexity of machinery for
international co-operation between the wars should be emphasized: for in addition to the large number of League
agencies, the I.L.O. and the Permanent Court of International Justice, the Pan American Union and the Commonwealth each built up a large number of organs. The latter
includes such organizations as the Commonwealth Agricultural Bureaux, the Scientific Liaison Offices, the Shipping
Committee, the Air Transport Council, etc. In these years
older organizations developed and flourished: e.g. the Bureau
of Information for the Universities of the Empire dated from
1912, was consolidated in 1919, and after 1932 became the
body known (since 1948) as the Association of Universities of
the British Commonwealth.

the time, it is important to notice that both these reasons were operative. The principles of international co-operation on which the League was based may be summarized as three:

(i) The principle of the sovereign equality of all member states, as expressed in their equality of voting power in the General Assembly, and the requirement of unanimity for all important decisions made by that body (Articles 1, 3, and 5);

(ii) The principle that each member state would refrain from going to war until all other means (diplomatic negotiation, arbitration, and submission of a dispute to the Council of the League) had been used and had failed to settle the dispute: embodied in Articles 12–14.

(iii) The principle that each member state would help to defend any other member state which became a victim of aggression, commonly called the principle of 'collective security', and embodied in Articles 10–11 and 15–17.

The first principle—that states should deal with one another on terms of 'sovereign equality'—was equally a principle of both the Pan American Union and the British Commonwealth. Not only was this principle emphasized by the separate membership of all the constituent members, at one time or another, in the League of Nations: but each group specifically stated the principle in relation to its own organizations. The Charter of the Organization of the American States, signed at the Conference at Bogota in 1948, echoed the traditions of half a century when it stated (Art. 6) that 'States are juridically equal, enjoy equal rights and equal capacity to exercise these rights, and have equal duties.'[1] The Balfour Report of 1926 stated that 'equality of status, so far as Great Britain and the Dominions are concerned, is . . . the root principle of our inter-imperial relations'. But within the framework of such juridical equality there existed, in all three organizations, a real inequality of power. Within the Pan American bodies it was always clear that the United States was the major partner, and that the success of the organizations depended largely on how far she was able to co-operate with the major Latin American powers of Argentina and Brazil. Within the Commonwealth it was recognized in 1926 that 'the principles of equality and similarity, appropriate to *status*, do not universally extend to function,' and the leadership of the London government was generally accepted. Successful international co-operation would seem to depend on simultaneous recognition of juridical equality and equality of consideration with recognition of functional differentiation and capacities of leadership. It was here that the League differed most fundamentally from its two collateral organizations, both in its formal structure and in its habits of operation.

A corollary of sovereign equality as a principle is that the international organizations resting thereon are

---

[1] The names have changed several times, but the substance remains largely identical: the Inter-American Conference of 1889–90 gave birth to the Pan American Union, this to the Inter-American System, and this in 1948 to the Organization of American States.

voluntary in nature. All three recognized this by accepting the right of withdrawal at will. But the readiness of states to exercise this right—and with it the rights of neutrality in the event of war—depended on the degree to which they had faith in the ability of the organization to guarantee their security. Because this faith stood highest within the Commonwealth, and higher within the Pan American organizations than within the League, the number of withdrawals from the League was very much greater than from either of the others.

The second principle, that all other means of settling disputes should be exhausted before recourse be had to war, similarly depended upon how far states were willing to treat inequalities of power as irrelevant to such disputes. Because of their common traditions and their common interest in preserving the unity of the Commonwealth, the members of the Commonwealth regarded no dispute between them as important enough to be worth recourse to war. The American states, with the few exceptions mentioned, shared a similar attitude. The more disparate and diversified members of the League did not share this view, and to the aggressive dictators in particular the collapse of the League was essential for achieving their ambitions.

Likewise, as regards the third principle on which the League rested, that of collective security, the actual interdependence of nations was less than the apostles of internationalism had assumed, and the extent to which there was actual interdependence was less fully appreciated than the successful operation of the system of collective security required. The Japanese invasion

of Manchuria and the Italian attack on Abyssinia were
not felt, by either the governments or the majorities of
the peoples of most other members of the League, to
constitute so direct a threat to their separate national
interests as to warrant the supreme sanction of recourse to war against the aggressors. And even in 1938
the British Prime Minister could defend his failure to
help preserve the independence of Czechoslovakia on
the grounds that it was 'a far away country of which we
know nothing'.

In these ways the League was left without any
general acceptance of its essential principles, and it suffered total collapse as a means of preserving the peace
of the world. By the nineteen-thirties the interests of
its leading members were sufficiently divergent for its
principles to be without solid foundation: and they were,
in this sense, inapplicable in the conditions of the time.
States sought refuge in less universal but more cohesive groupings, such as the Commonwealth and the
Pan American Union, wherein they accepted a more
real community of interests. International relations
suffered from the working of a vicious circle, in which
changing conditions made the principles of the League
increasingly inapplicable, and realization of this fact
made members increasingly unwilling to try to apply
them. The nations of the world were not ready for uni-
versalism of the kind implied in the Covenant: just as
the World Economic Conference of 1933, at which 64
countries were represented, served little purpose but to
prove that the world's economic ills could not be cured
by any simple ecumenical formula.

In consequence, international relations relapsed to a state of incoherence. There remained no machinery capable of preventing, deterring, or punishing aggression; no faith in the ability or even the desire of nation-states to keep the peace; no system of clear national interests resting on reliable alliances or even a balance of power in the world. It was not only that none felt that other states could be relied on to keep their promises; they could not even be relied on to pursue their own interests coherently and with strength of purpose. Crucial nations were deeply divided internally about what their interests were: so that France was led to neglect what was so plainly and traditionally a national interest as the demilitarization of the Rhineland, and Poland could be induced to deny the basis of her own national interests to the extent of sharing in the dismemberment of Czechoslovakia. Nations most naturally interested in preserving the settlement of 1919 were torn internally between a policy of resistance to dictatorship and a policy of 'appeasement'; a word which in the nineteen-thirties lost the soothing and constructive sense it had enjoyed in the nineteen-twenties, and acquired instead a tone of defeatism and surrender. The new diplomacy of open conferences broke down, yet there was no frank recourse to the old diplomacy or clear systems of alliances. By 1939 there existed a shell of international organization not animated by faith or will, a series of improvised alliances uncemented by any consolidation of interests or common plans, and a balance of power in the world strongly in favour of the rearmed and re-solute dictatorships.

Even so, war came in 1939 not because any state wanted war for its own sake. All nations regarded it as a calamity and even the most aggressive leaders posed as having been long-suffering in the cause of peace. There had been widespread relief when war was avoided at Munich; Mussolini, who had praised war as putting 'the stamp of nobility upon the peoples who have the courage to meet it', was careful not to meet war with France until she was beaten; and even Hitler, whose personal inclinations and political position probably impelled him towards war, felt obliged to make much of his efforts for peaceful settlements and of the 'warlike' policies of his opponents. War came because some governments (especially those of Germany and Japan) wanted to attain ends for which they were prepared to pay the price of war, and because they had been encouraged to believe that the cost of war would not be too heavy; and also because other governments and nations, though ill-prepared for war, were at last so determined to stop them that they, too, were willing to pay the price of war which they knew from the start would be heavy. In the result, the price that each side had to pay was all the heavier, and every pre-war policy was discredited. Aggression did not pay Germany or Italy or Japan, for all were defeated. Appeasement did not save Britain and France from going to war. The neutrality of Belgium did not save her from invasion, nor did United States neutrality keep her out of war. The Nazi-Soviet Pact of 1939 did not spare the Soviet Union the German onslaught of 1941. Nor did the vast amount of constructive international co-operation achieved at a technical and functional level by the many voluntary and special agencies succeed in creating that nexus of common national interests which its exponents hoped might create peace by creating an international community. The second world war was one of the greatest failures of human intelligence and organization in world history.

Chapter Five
THE SECOND WORLD WAR, 1939–1945

§1. *Issues Involved*

THE second world war, like the first, began ostensibly about a quarrel concerning national minorities in eastern Europe. In March and April 1939 Hitler made demands on Poland for the incorporation of Danzig into German territory and the concession of a road and rail connexion across the Polish province of Pomorze. The Polish government refused, and after a farce of German ultimatums which it was given no chance to meet, the German armies invaded Poland on 1 September 1939. Great Britain, having guaranteed in March to defend Poland against such an attack, declared war on Germany and was joined within a week by all the Dominions except Eire. France, being also pledged to defend Poland, within six hours likewise declared war on Germany. Until Italy declared war on France and Britain in June 1940 no other state entered the war except those which Germany invaded and occupied as a prelude to her attack on France in the spring of 1940 (i.e. Norway, Belgium, and the Netherlands). Denmark, though occupied, did not become a belligerent state. The first phase of the war, prior to the collapse of France in June 1940, was thus limited in scope both territorially and politically. It was not, in a strict sense, a world war, although the entry of the Commonwealth made it affect to some degree every continent in the world. It was still essentially a European war—a contest to restrain the Nazi dictatorship of Germany from dominating the continent of Europe: and as such, by the time the British were driven from Dunkirk and the French government signed the armistices with Germany and Italy in June 1940, it had failed to prevent German hegemony in Europe. By that date Germany controlled the whole of Austria, Czechoslovakia, Denmark, Norway, Belgium, the Netherlands, half Poland, and most of France. The western coasts of Europe, from the Arctic to the Bay of Biscay were in German hands. No British troops remained on the continent.

But the circumstances in which war began indicated much greater and more world-wide upheavals. In August 1939 the Soviet Union entered into a pact with Germany whereby Germany acquiesced in Russian annexation of the three Baltic states of Lithuania, Latvia, and Estonia, part of Poland, and a strip of Finland. Three months later the Soviet Union launched an invasion of Finland, and for so doing was expelled from the League of Nations in December. But by March 1940 Finland was compelled to cede various southern parts of her territory. Russian forces also occupied the eastern (and larger) part of Poland. These concerted aggressions betokened the final collapse of the settlement of 1919 and the opening of a new era in European history. Much would henceforth hinge on the relations between the partners of the Nazi-Soviet Pact: sharply opposed in ideology and by long national traditions, clearly in considerable conflict of interests both economic and strategic, yet temporarily in agreement to secure mutual advantages at the expense of other states. But the immediate future hung on whether or not Germany could achieve her objective of either inducing Great Britain to make an armistice, or conquering her by aerial bombardment and invasion. The Battle of Britain, fought in the skies during the late summer of 1940, determined that the Commonwealth would make no truce with Germany.

It meant, accordingly, that the war in the west, mainly on sea and in the air, would continue into 1941: and the proclaimed aims of Germany's 'new order' in Europe, which she forthwith began to implement in the occupied countries, ensured that the war now became one for national survival, against a régime of racial discrimination and domination by the 'master race'. The issues during this phase were clear enough. German treatment of the Poles, who as Slavs were treated as an inferior race to be subjected utterly to the needs and interests of the Germans, and of the Jews, whose extermination was an essential goal of Nazi ideology, made it a war for nationalism against racialism. The establishment of single-party puppet régimes in most of the occupied countries also made it a war for democratic freedoms against fascist tyranny. The election of President Roosevelt for a third term in 1940 ensured that United States influence and—so far as Congress and public opinion would allow—her economic and diplomatic assistance, would be thrown on to the British side in this contest. This phase ended sharply with Germany's attack on the Soviet Union in June 1941.

M

The war was now less clearly one of democracies against single-party régimes, since the Soviet Union at once became an ally of the democracies. It remained one of nationalism against racialism and German hegemony, because the Red Army fought to repel a foreign invader from Russian soil. And now that Germany was engaged in a war on two fronts and her original strategy of *Blitzkrieg* had failed, she was doomed to suffer very heavy losses both from aerial bombardment from the west and in land fighting on the eastern front. By the end of 1941 the defence of Moscow marked the failure of the German *Blitzkrieg* in the east. By its policy of 'scorched earth', reminiscent of Russian tactics against Napoleon in 1812, the Soviet Union bought time with space and inflicted very heavy losses on the German armies. The industries beyond the Urals, supplemented by supplies shipped or flown to Russia by her western allies, kept the Red Army supplied.

On 7 December the action of Japan in bombing every United States and British base within reach, converted the war into a world war. In July she had absorbed French Indo-China. The losses she now inflicted on the American fleet at Pearl Harbour, and on the British by sinking the battleship *Prince of Wales* and the battle-cruiser *Repulse*, gave her naval supremacy in the Pacific and in the waters of East Asia. She used this supremacy to conquer, at great speed, Hong Kong, Malaya, Singapore, the Dutch East Indies and Borneo, the Philippines, the Andamans, and Burma. Four days after the attack on Pearl Harbour Germany and Italy declared war on the United States, and the war encircled the globe. Every great power was henceforth engaged, and every continent and every ocean of the world became a theatre of operations. The alignment of forces was now that of the 'Anti-Comintern Pact'— Germany, Italy, and Japan—against a world coalition of powers, led by Britain and the United States, and including the Soviet Union and China, which had been in a state of war with Japan since 1937. The German ambition of establishing a new order in Europe was matched by the Japanese ambition of setting up a vast dominion in Asia and the Pacific: and each had made large conquests. There was one significant link missing in the chain. Despite her adhesion to the Anti-Comintern Pact Japan was not at war with the Soviet Union. It was not until after Germany's defeat in 1945, and within a few days of Japan's surrender, that the Soviet Union declared war on Japan.

This fact is a warning against regarding ideological issues as decisive in the alignment of forces. Each state acted on careful calculation of its separate national interests, and it is noteworthy that neither the Soviet Union nor the United States engaged in war until it became the victim of aggression. The sharpest conflicts of ideology were brushed aside when they cut across national interests: by the Soviet Union when it made the Nazi-Soviet Pact in 1939, by Great Britain when she welcomed the Soviet Union as her ally in 1941, by Japan when she refrained from attacking the Soviet Union. But, just as in the first world war, the experience of war and the necessities of conducting modern warfare stimulated governments and peoples alike to formulate war aims and peace aims in ideological terms. The growth of organized resistance movements in the occupied countries of Europe and the Far East led to a crystallization of objectives, and the campaigns of liberation in 1944 and 1945 were accompanied by programmes of reconstruction. The conduct of psychological warfare, by radio and leaflet, against enemy countries required some basis in political theory. The need to sustain morale on the home front, in face of great social upheaval and often heavy civilian casualties from bombing, led to formulation of post-war aims and ideals. Men everywhere had to know what they were fighting for if they were to go on fighting at all: and although the basic appeal remained that of nationalism —of national independence and self-government—this was found to be inadequate in itself. It was increasingly supplemented by the appeal of socialism, and the 'socializing of nationalism' was greatly extended by the war.[1]

The first systematic formulation of war aims was the Atlantic Charter, drawn up by Mr. Churchill and President Roosevelt on 14 August 1941, before the alignment of states already described had fully come into being. Their aim was to state 'certain common principles in the national policies of their respective countries on which they base their hopes for a better future for the world'. The burden of the eight points in which they summarized these common principles was preservation of national sovereignty and independence, combined with international co-operation to

[1] In the broad sense described above, Chapter IV, §2.

promote economic prosperity, disarmament, and peace. But they also mentioned 'the object of securing for all improved labour standards, economic advancement, and social security,' and assurance of 'freedom from fear and want'.[1] A month later the exiled allied governments in London (Belgium, Czechoslovakia, Greece, Luxemburg, the Netherlands, Norway, Poland, Yugoslavia) as well as the Free French and the Soviet Union, endorsed this statement of purposes. It was still further endorsed in Article VII of the Mutual Aid agreement between Britain and the United States in February 1942 and repeated in subsequent Lend-lease agreements with the Soviet Union, China, Ethiopia, Liberia, Australia, Canada, and New Zealand. It was reiterated in the Anglo-Soviet Treaty of May 1942. The joint four-nations declaration on general security, issued after the Moscow Conference of October 1943 on behalf of the United Kingdom, the United States, the Soviet Union, and China, emphasized nationalism almost exclusively. It spoke of the need to set up 'a general international organization, based on the principle of the sovereign equality of all peace-loving States'. Subsequent joint declarations at Cairo (November 1943), Teheran (December 1943), and Yalta (February 1945) were primarily concerned with the conduct of the war and the immediate political

---

[1] For the texts of this and subsequent declarations, see *United Nations Documents, 1941-1945,* published (1946) by the Royal Institute of International Affairs. President Roosevelt, in his speech of January 1941 after his election for a third term, included 'freedom from want and fear' as two of the 'four essential freedoms'.

problems of post-war settlement. They were also framed in basically nationalistic terms.

But the ideals of social security, economic democracy, and freedom from want were powerfully stated in a series of separate declarations, and were recognized as an objective of international organization in the constitution of various new United Nations agencies. In May 1944 the General Conference of the International Labour Organization, meeting in Philadelphia and representing forty-one member countries, issued a statement of 'the principles which should inspire the policy of its members'. It is the most remarkable statement of a fusion of the ideals of nationalism and socialism ever issued with such world-wide support. Its basic principle is that 'all human beings, irrespective of race, creed, or sex, have the right to pursue both their material well-being and their spiritual development in conditions of freedom and dignity, of economic security and equal opportunity', and it declares that 'the attainment of the conditions in which this shall be possible must constitute the central aim of national and international policy'. It then lists ten specific objectives calculated to produce such conditions. These include 'full employment and the raising of standards of living', 'policies in regard to wages and earnings, hours and other conditions of work calculated to ensure a just share of the fruits of progress to all, and a minimum living wage to all employed and in need of such protection', 'the extension of social security measures to provide a basic income to all in need of such protection and comprehensive medical care', 'adequate protection for the life and health of workers in all occupations', 'provision for child welfare and maternity protection', 'the provision of adequate nutrition, housing, and facilities for recreation and culture', and 'the assurance of equality of educational and vocational opportunity'. Once again the warfare state gave powerful impetus to the growth of the welfare state.

Internationally a series of agencies was set up to tackle by concerted action both immediate and more long-term economic and social problems. In 1943 the United Nations Relief and Rehabilitation Administration (U.N.R.R.A.) was set up to deal with immediate relief work. In 1945 the Food and Agriculture Organization was created to concert action in raising standards of nutrition, improving methods of production and distribution of foodstuffs, bettering the condition of rural populations, and 'thus contributing towards an expanding world economy'. Financial and currency problems, hinging on international credit facilities, were to be the concern of the International Monetary Fund and the International Bank for Reconstruction and Development devised at Bretton Woods in 1944 on the basis of proposals made by Lord Keynes and by Mr. H. D. White of the United States. Wider social and cultural co-operation was the task of the United Nations Educational, Scientific, and Cultural Organization (U.N.E.S.C.O.). The preamble to its constitution included the remarkable words, 'since wars begin in the minds of men, it is in the minds of men that the defences of peace must be constructed', and declared that peace must be founded 'upon the intellectual and moral solidarity of mankind'.

Through these and other measures[1] the ideals and aspirations generated by the fighting of the war were reduced from manifestos and words to concrete and elaborate international organizations. They were matched, on a domestic level, by new national plans. In 1942 the Beveridge *Report on Social Insurance and Allied Services* had appeared in Britain, and the plan for social security which it outlined was widely discussed both nationally and internationally. Two years later appeared its sequel on *Full Employment in a Free Society*. The war-time and post-war governments, particularly the Labour Government which ruled with a large majority from 1945 until 1950, implemented most of the projects for educational reorganization, a national health service, family allowances, social security and nationalization which had been prepared during the war. In March 1944 the National Council of Resistance in France, representing the main internal resistance movements, drew up a 'Resistance Charter'. It set out the measures to be taken after liberation to secure 'a more just social order' and 'a true economic and social democracy'. These included 'a complete plan for social security', nationalization of the main means of

---

[1] The number and diversity of international agencies set up at this time preclude their full consideration here: their activities may conveniently be studied in *International Conciliation*, published by the *Carnegie Endowment for International Peace*. All depended for their success on the voluntary co-operation of national governments, and none constituted a federalist or supra-national authority such as the later Schuman Plan, discussed below (Chapter VI, §1.)

production and credit, and security of employment. In 1945 it was accepted by all the major political parties as a programme for reconstruction, and the provisional governments, resting on a strong coalition of Communists, Socialists, and Catholic Democrats, proceeded to introduce measures of nationalization, family allowances, pensions, and social welfare. The later Monnet Plan, for modernizing and re-equipping the national economy, was the most systematic piece of economic and social planning known in French history.

The prolonged and desperate character of the struggle in itself affected, in these ways, the world's conception of the issues at stake. All the United Nations, so long as they constituted a grand alliance against the aggressive dictatorships, could agree that the first purpose of victory was to destroy the dictators and the despotic régimes which they had established in occupied countries. All were obliged to promise themselves and others a restoration of national independence and sovereign rights together with a new international system to make possible closer co-operation in the tasks of the post-war years. They were also led, though with varying degrees of emphasis, to justify this reassertion of nationalism by endorsing the ideals of social welfare and security for all men. Haunted by the experience of world economic crisis and mass unemployment which had followed the first world war, they were conscious of the need to prevent a repetition of the economic depression which had bred and fed the movements of fascism. The enormous growth of state control and detailed regulation of everyday life, which were the inevitable accompaniments of modern warfare, accustomed people everywhere to governmental action for the common good. The tendencies apparent in the first world war were now greatly accentuated and extended: and aims such as social security 'from the cradle to the grave' and the maintenance of full employment called for a more continuous and far-reaching state organization than had been contemplated in the first world war. Everything conspired to make the national community into a highly socialized community, with its economic activities and its social life more profoundly than ever a concern of national governments. Long-term economic planning became the accepted instrument of the state.[1]

Behind the mixture of nationalistic and socialistic issues lay two other kinds of issue, less constantly in the minds of the belligerents but both of immense importance for the future of the world. One was determination of the whole balance of power-relations in the main oceans of the world. Were Britain and France, rather than Italy and Germany, to remain the dominant powers in the Mediterranean? Were the United States and Britain, rather than Germany, to remain the dominant powers in the Atlantic? Was the British Commonwealth to retain the Indian Ocean as one great focus of its existence, or was that area to be divided between India and Japan to the exclusion of the British? Was the hegemony of the Pacific to fall to Japan rather than to the United States? The victories of the United Na-

[1] Even of the United States: see *A Post-War Plan and Program for the U.S.A.*, issued in 1943 by the National Resources Planning Board.

tions determined all these issues in favour of the allies. Behind this issue lay another, even more far-reaching in its implications. Were the overseas empires of the white nations to remain in some colonial relationship with Europe, or were they to move towards complete independence? In many of them, movements and even concessions making for greater self-government and independence had existed before the war. The striking defeats of the white governments by the Japanese and, in most areas, the subsequent occupation of the colonial territories by the Japanese, transformed the whole situation. The position of the British in Singapore, Malaya, Burma, could never be the same again. Nor could the position of the Dutch in Indonesia, the French in Indo-China, even the Chinese in Manchuria. The upheaval in Europe had similar repercussions in the whole continent of Africa, affecting the position of the French in Algeria, Tunisia, and Morocco, the Italians in Libya, the British in Egypt, the Belgians in the Congo. A major consequence of the war was a colonial revolution projecting far into the future; and if the first world war had killed dynastic imperialism, it was probable that the second was a death-blow to colonial imperialism.

. . . . .

There also emerged from the course of the war a new conception of special importance and interest for world history: the systematic trial of war criminals, including not only those who had committed offences against the accepted rules of war but also those charged with 'crimes against humanity' and with 'crimes against peace', by planning or waging 'aggressive war'. From 1940 onwards allied governments had frequently protested against German treatment of the inhabitants of occupied countries, and by 1945 they were all committed to ensuring the trial and punishment of 'the major criminals whose offences have no particular geographical location', as well as of those who had committed atrocities. In the United States Justice Robert H. Jackson of the Supreme Court prepared a report to the President which, as a result of negotiations with the allies, led to the establishment of the International Military Tribunal. The principles behind the arrangements were stated like this:

In untroubled times, progress towards an effective rule of law in the international community is slow indeed. Inertia rests more heavily upon the society of nations than upon any other society. Now we stand at one of those rare moments when the thought and institutions and habits of the world have been shaken by the impact of world war on the lives of countless millions. Such occasions rarely come and quickly pass. We are put under a heavy responsibility to see that our behaviour during this unsettled period will direct the world's thought toward a firmer enforcement of the laws of international conduct, so as to make war less attractive to those who have governments and the destinies of peoples in their power.[1]

An international tribunal, including judges and prosecutors from the four major powers which instituted it (the United States, Great Britain, the Soviet Union, and France), was duly set up at Nuremberg, and in-

[1] Justice Jackson's original report (*U.S. Department of State, Publication 3080*, pp. 42–54,) became the main basis for the procedure and organization at Nuremberg.

dictments were filed against 24 individuals and 6 groups or organizations. The individuals included Hermann Goering, Rudolf Hess, von Ribbentrop, and von Neurath amongst political leaders, Admirals Raeder and Doenitz and Generals Keitel and Jodl among service chiefs, and such leading administrators as Ley, Frick, Sauckel, and Speer; the organizations included the Reich Cabinet, the General Staff and High Command, and the Gestapo.

Trials of former enemy leaders on this scale before an international tribunal were without precedent. It is noteworthy that the rules of procedure were a blend of the different legal systems of the four countries concerned. Defendants were allowed to take the witness stand and testify subject to cross-examination, as is customary in English and American criminal procedure but not in continental legal systems; they were also allowed to make statements to the tribunal not under oath and not subject to cross-examination, as is customary in continental practice but not in English or American. The proceedings, despite the great difficulties of language and technicality, were in general conducted with a dignity and judicial propriety which were not always notable at the other national trials of alleged traitors. The sentences were not excessive and were even open to the criticism that they were too light, considering the gravity of the offences; two of the defendants were acquitted. Nor could the judgements be described as hasty; trials continued until 1949. More serious was the criticism that the judges included representatives of the Soviet Union, which had been expelled from the League of Nations in 1939 because of its aggression against Finland, which had invaded Poland as Germany's ally in 1939, and which countenanced concentration-camps and forced labour camps not notably different in nature from those now condemned in Nazi Germany. It was widely felt that this circumstance greatly weakened the purpose of the trials, which was to condemn impartially such actions as had made the second world war possible and which had then made its conduct so savage; and to make progress towards the ideal of world order under the 'rule of law'. Similar trials were held of Japanese 'war criminals', and local military tribunals of the occupying powers tried those accused of local offences. In all thousands of persons were so brought to trial. It seems likely that such judicial action is now established as a proper and almost inevitable aftermath of a major war, and this at least is an important new fact in world history, likely to strengthen rather than weaken the force of international law. As an eminent American prosecutor at Nuremberg has put it, 'Nuremberg is a historical and moral fact with which, from now on, every government must reckon in its internal and external policies alike.'[1]

§2. *The Burden of War*

> War lays a burden on the reeling state,
> And peace does nothing to relieve the weight.

So wrote William Cowper, and before considering

[1] Telford Taylor: *The Nuremberg War Crimes Trials* (*International Conciliation*, No. 450, April, 1949, p. 352.)

further the plans of peace 'to relieve the weight', it is
well to assess the burden of the war. The most striking
feature of the course of the war was the speed and the
sweeping extent of German and Japanese victories
during the first half of the war, and the equally dramatic
and shattering successes of the allies during the second
half. The whole war lasted from 1 September 1939,
when Germany invaded Poland, until 2 September
1945, when Japan formally surrendered to the allied
forces. It thus lasted six years and a day. Until November 1942 most of the advantages and gains lay with
Germany and Japan: after that month, which saw the
victories of El Alamein and Stalingrad, the disembarka-
tion of allied forces in French North Africa, and the
establishment of United States forces on Guadalcanal
in the Solomons, the tide turned and a long series of
allied advances began which ended in the liberation of
western Europe and of south-east Asia, and the surrender of Germany and Japan.

There are reasons for this clear-cut pattern which lie
in the very nature of modern warfare and in the relative
resources of the combatants. More than any previous
war, it was a war of machines: of aircraft and tanks,
motorized columns and heavy artillery, ships and submarines. Such instruments of war are, in their nature,
products of great scientific inventiveness and technical
skill, and depend for their manufacture in adequate
quantities upon the methods of mass production. Such
resources are normally available only in the larger and
most highly industrialized countries. Upon the equipment of states with a supply of up-to-date weapons

sufficient to engage in war the methods of mass-production impose two severe limitations. One is that before the plant needed to produce a flow of tanks or aircraft can operate, a time-lag of between one and two years must elapse whilst the machines to make the machines (known as machine-tools and jigs) are themselves being manufactured. The other is that, once such plant has been set up, the form of weapons it produces cannot be changed in important respects without causing further delays and a sharp decline in output. The problem of building up armaments to maximum strength can only be solved, therefore, in relation to the exact time when operations of war will begin. If a government begins mass production too early, it may find its stores of equipment out of date: if it begins too late, its output will be too small. This fact gives an immense initial advantage to an aggressor, who can fix the date when war will begin to coincide with his own maximum and optimum production of the weapons of war. This advantage was fully and skilfully utilized by both Germany and Japan, and very largely explained their great successes in the first three years. The speed of the Polish campaign (three weeks) and of the French (six weeks), the concentrated ferocity of the German advance into Russia, which within six months carried the German armies to the gates of Leningrad and Sevastopol and brought them within sight of Moscow, the impetus of the Japanese offensive which in three months won them Malaya, Singapore, Burma, the Philippines, and Netherlands East Indies, are all manifestations of this technical advantage.

But the factors of both superior resources of man-power and greater industrial potential were, if appropriately used, on the side of the United Nations. France and Great Britain had delayed their programmes of re-armament so much that their output could not, during the first year of the war, compete in bulk with Germany's. But by the end of 1941 Britain's output was reaching its target, and the mass-production resources of the Soviet Union were brought into the balance against Germany. Above all the vast resources of the United States, even before her entry as a belligerent, had become increasingly available to Britain through the devices of 'cash-and-carry' and (after March 1941) of 'Lend-lease'. In May 1940 the United States had begun a big rearmament programme, and President Roosevelt had warned Congress that the country should be 'geared up to the ability to produce at least 50,000 planes a year'. It was inevitable that, by the end of 1942, the total advantage in war should swing in favour of the allies. At the peak of its output in 1943-1944, the United States was producing one ship a day and one aircraft every five minutes. President Roosevelt had spoken of his country as 'the arsenal of the democracies'. In the six years of war that arsenal produced 87,000 tanks, 296,000 aircraft, 315,000 pieces of artillery and mortars, 2,434,000 trucks, and 53,000,000 tons of shipping.

For the main belligerents, then, the first burden of war was the complete reorganization of their industrial production to mass-produce the equipment of war. This was accompanied, in all save the overseas Dominions and the United States, by immense material destruction:

N

in the United Kingdom, France, Germany, and Japan by concentrated aerial bombing, in all the occupied countries, the Soviet Union, and Germany by armed invasion. At sea the destruction of shipping by mines, submarines, surface ships, and aircraft reached a level unknown in the first world war. Total allied losses exceeded 20,000,000 tons; but this, as shown above could be much more than replaced by United States shipbuilding resources. Each belligerent, however, suffered from moments of crisis when it seemed that, in the race for production, output was lagging behind consumption. In the winter of 1941–1942 the bulk of the German army was strewn over the vast 'scorched' areas of western Russia, its lines of communication stretched to the utmost and its men suffering from one of the worst winters in living memory. At that moment Germany experienced a production crisis because her stocks had dwindled, her plant was getting worn, food was scarce, and she suffered from an acute shortage of skilled labour. It was a crisis reminiscent of 1916, and was tackled by the Nazi Party with an emergency programme directed by Albert Speer, with the help of Fritz Sauckel as director of labour allocation. During 1942 the whole of occupied Europe was combed for fresh supplies of labour and millions of workers were transported to German factories. But the heavy losses of 1942 culminated in the defeat of Stalingrad, where Germany lost the 350,000 men of her Sixth Army; and Sauckel's 'total mobilization' of January 1943 was a measure of the continuing crisis of production. By then aerial bombardment, too, was slowing down vital production, and the country was feeling the effects of the dreaded 'war on two fronts'. Japan underwent a similar crisis, and for the same reasons, in the winter of 1944–1945.

Strategy for the most effective use of the equipment hinged on a systematic accumulation of it to the point when overwhelming weight and superiority made possible a concentrated and irresistible attack. This was the classical method used by the aggressor states in preparing their initial surprise attacks, and it was equally the method adopted by the allies in their counter-offensives. The campaigns in North Africa afforded more than one example of this method. Success depended on the exact co-ordination of the different categories of weapon: armoured power on land, air power combined with it, and both, wherever possible, concerted with the appropriate use of sea power. It was skilful use of such combined operations which carried Rommel's Afrika Korps up to Tobruk in the first two months of 1942, and on to El Alamein by June, in his campaign to capture Egypt and the Middle East. It was even more skilful use of it which enabled General Montgomery's Eighth Army to repulse Rommel at El Alamein and in October 1942 to drive the Afrika Korps back along the coast road harried by aerial and naval bombardment. An artillery barrage from 1,000 guns had opened the attack, in a manner reminiscent of the offensives on the western front in the first world war. The Germans lost 60,000 men in the battle.

But losses of life on this scale in battle, except on the vast Russian front, were rare in the second world war.

The hopes of the builders of the French Maginot Line, that scientific and mechanized warfare could be thrifty in lives, were partially fulfilled though not in the way they had expected. The very concentration and speed of most major operations meant that usually more men were taken prisoners than were killed. A war of movement avoided the long and deadly periods of attrition, followed by holocausts of life, which had marked the first war. France, which was twice a major battlefield and was throughout subject to air attack, lost some 500,000 lives, including those killed in the resistance: a third of her losses in the first war. The United States, which had over 12,000,000 troops engaged, suffered losses of some 325,000; the British Commonwealth and Empire forces lost, in killed and missing, nearly 445,000, of which well over half came from the United Kingdom alone.

But the defeated powers, and the Soviet Union which suffered heavy initial reverses on land, lost lives on a scale even exceeding that of the first war. Germany lost 2,250,000 combatants killed in battle. Japan, which was at war continuously from 1937 until 1945, lost in all some 1,174,000, and in addition 330,000 civilians killed in air-raids, of whom 92,000 were killed at Hiroshima. The losses of Russia have even been alleged to exceed 15,000,000, but no reliable figures are available and both sides had a certain interest in exaggerating the Russian losses. It seems probable that, in the course of the whole war, the total number of civilians killed exceeded the number of people killed in uniform. In the United Kingdom, over 60,000 civilians were killed by bombs and rockets. It was, as never before, a war between whole nations, and women and children figured very high in the death-rolls. In the east, when all was over, the highest figures were for those just 'missing'. The war of rapid movement made conceptions of 'fronts' almost inapplicable, and concentration on bombing of 'the home front' made it as important a theatre of war as any other. The German theory of 'the Nation in Arms' had triumphed in the first war: in the second it was replaced by the very different principle of 'the Nation at War'.

A further characteristic was the enormous displacement of people. From the start the Germans, in Poland and France, used the hordes of civilian refugees as a means of confusing and embarrassing the enemy. Bombing rendered millions homeless. The favourite precaution, evacuation, still meant displacement. Hitler's New Order and German conscription of labour in the occupied countries transferred millions of Europeans from their homes. Each side took millions of prisoners. On the eastern European front the ebb and flow of the tide of battle wiped out thousands of towns and villages. The refugee, exile, prisoner of war, and displaced person were the victims of modern war. They bequeathed to the post-war world a vast problem of resettlement and rehousing, which the division of Germany and the reshaping of the map in eastern Europe and the Middle East made still more intractable.

With the massive destruction, death, dislocation and uprooting went, inevitably, starvation and fabulous indebtedness. It was supremely fortunate that the world's richest resources, in the United States and the overseas Dominions, were left untouched by the destructiveness of war. America's capacity to produce food and goods, and ships to transport them, combined with her remarkable willingness to do everything within her power to set world economy on its feet again, saved the world from even worse horrors of starvation. By the mechanism of 'Lend-lease' during the war and of 'Marshall Aid' after the war, Europe and large parts of the east were kept supplied with necessities until they could again produce more for themselves. 'Stopgap' aid of $597,000,000 approved by the Interim Aid Act which passed through the United States Congress in December 1947 was followed in April 1948 by the Foreign Assistance Act. This provided $5,300,000,000 for the first year of a 'European Recovery Programme', $465,000,000 for China and $275,000,000 for Turkey and Greece. But for such measures it seems certain that acute scarcity in Europe and the Far East would have been accompanied, within a few years of the end of the war, by an economic depression in the United States. American productive capacity was kept geared at its high war-time level for providing aid to much of the rest of the world. Meanwhile U.N.R.R.A. and its successor, the International Refugee Organization (I.R.O.), gave essential first-aid to the most stricken countries of the world.

The extent to which it was truly a 'world war' may be measured by the small number of states which contrived to remain neutral throughout, though in most cases their sympathy for the allied cause was obvious

enough. Turkey and Spain were induced to curtail their
exports of rare metals to Germany, Sweden and Switzerland clung to their traditional roles as the servants of
humanitarian causes and played a valuable part as inter-
mediaries for Red Cross and postal activities, Portugal
agreed to lease bases in the Azores to Britain. Egypt
remained a neutral state much more in name than in
reality. No South American state remained neutral
throughout, although Argentina did not become a belligerent until March 1945. Eire permitted individual
volunteers to join the British forces whilst denying the
use of her ports to the allies. The United Nations,
although excluding former enemy powers, was thus
from the outset a more universal body than the Allied
and Associated Powers of 1919.

§3. *New Balance of Power*

The course of events which began on 'D-Day' (6
June 1944) led to the liberation of all western European
countries and the defeat of Germany. A vast allied
army, under the supreme command of General Eisen-
hower, was landed in France in the most massive and
masterly combined operation in history. In one country
after another nations experienced the withdrawal or the
defeat of the German armies, and were confronted with
the common problems of setting up national governments of their own, reconstructing their economic life
and finding the path back to a more normal existence.
In some, such as Norway and the Netherlands, exiled
monarchs and governments could return and resume
national leadership, usually in co-operation with the

internal forces of resistance which had formed during enemy occupation. In others, such as France and Italy, where pre-war régimes had collapsed, new constitutional systems had to be devised. In all, the urgent needs of resettlement, reform, and reconstruction called for vigorous and firm governmental action, and no state could avoid assuming wide control over national social and economic life. Meanwhile the Red Army, advancing on a tottering Germany from the east, had likewise driven out the German forces from Poland, Czechoslovakia, and the Baltic states. Germany's Balkan satellites, Rumania, Bulgaria, and Hungary, underwent violent changes of régime and signed armistices with the Soviet Union. So, too, did Finland. British forces freed Greece and allied forces made their way, with heavy fighting, up the Italian peninsula, though it was 2 May 1945 before hostilities ended in Italy. In the west the last year of the war brought two examples of German resilience, even in face of inevitable defeat. From June 1944 until the western countries were liberated, thousands of rocket-bombs (V-1) followed by jet-propelled rockets (V-2) were launched against Britain, particularly London. It was autumn before they were checked by capture of the launching-sites. In December the German commander, von Runstedt, launched a remarkably powerful counter-attack on the Rhine which caught the United States forces by surprise and led to the 'battle of the bulge'. Prolonged resistance served no purpose but to demonstrate that the German armies were, this time, completely beaten, and on 7 May the High Command surrendered unconditionally.

Although many plans had been prepared for the re-habilitation of liberated countries and for the military government of enemy territories, it was still assumed that the war in the Far East might go on for many months more. As in 1918, the speedy end of the war caught the victorious allies by surprise. When Germany surrendered the United States had already reconquered the Philippines, British, United States, and Chinese forces had retaken Burma, and Japan was fighting a losing war in Okinawa. Japan was in a sorry plight, for she came under deadly bombardment from the air and a vast allied navy was preparing for full-scale invasion. But it was not impossible that, if the invasion planned for November had to be launched, there would still be many months of heavy fighting before the country was effectively occupied. The two atomic bombs, dropped on Hiroshima on 6 August and on Nagasaki three days later, compelled Japan to surrender on 14 August. In the Far East, as in Europe, men were suddenly confronted with immense problems of reconstruction: but now overshadowed by the terrifying vista of new potentialities of destruction should the tasks of making peace be fumbled.

No power was more taken by surprise than the Soviet Union. It had delayed declaring war on Japan until two days after the bomb fell on Hiroshima. It was clear that its leaders had been unaware of the decisive results which could be obtained by this latest product of western science and technology. The dramatic climax to the six years of war—this thunderbolt as the clock was striking twelve—brought new fears and tensions between the Soviet Union and her western allies. At the conference at Yalta, held in February 1945, President Roosevelt and Mr. Churchill had agreed, in substance, to considerable concessions to Stalin in return for his promise to enter the war against Japan. At that time Soviet co-operation had seemed worth the price, though the price was high. It had included Soviet control of Manchurian ports and railroads, Communist preponderance in Poland and the Balkans, outside Greece and Italy, and the greatest share of reparations from Germany. Now it appeared that the price need not have been paid, for Soviet co-operation against Japan had been unnecessary. But Soviet forces held the whip hand in eastern Europe; and nothing effective could be done, in any case, to destroy their influence in a Europe where Germany was defeated and, after the agreement at Potsdam in July, divided into British, French, American, and Soviet zones of occupation. It was hoped that by May 1946 final peace treaties might be drawn up and signed. A conference which opened in Paris in July 1946 eventually framed treaties for Bulgaria, Rumania, Hungary, Finland and Italy. These were duly signed, but the most important problems, of a peace settlement with Germany, Austria and Japan, and of agreeing some general scheme of disarmament which now involved above all the control of atomic energy, were postponed until the era of the 'cold war' descended icily upon the former allies.

It was a feature of the post-war arrangements that of the leaders of the three major allies only Stalin survived in power. President Roosevelt died on 12 April 1945 and was succeeded by Harry S. Truman. Winston Churchill, who since he first became British Prime Minister in the darkest hour of May 1940 had been the inspiration of Commonwealth and European resistance to the Axis, fell from power in the general election of July 1945 and was succeeded by Mr. Attlee with a large Labour Party majority. The end of the war thus had to be conducted, among the western allies, by two men who were new to the very highest offices of power and decision: and it was they who attended the Potsdam conference in July, although Mr. Churchill was also there for its first stages. It was they, too, who became responsible for the rest of the peace settlement. In this respect treaty-making in 1945 was different from that of 1919, when it was the war-time leaders of the three victorious powers who also dominated the settlement. But there is little evidence that this change in personalities greatly affected the course of events or the nature of the decisions.

The virtual suspension of further peacemaking in 1947, and the onset of the period of 'cold war', perpetuated into the post-war years a new balance of power in the world. The hopes for a concert of power, similar to that which existed after 1815, were at first high. On such hopes rested the Council of Foreign Ministers responsible for making the peace treaties, the Allied Control Council for Germany, and the Security Council of the United Nations. On the latter the United States, the Soviet Union, United Kingdom, China, and France were each given a permanent seat and a veto-power. These hopes dwindled during 1946 and 1947, as each of

these institutions became an arena for increasingly
bitter wrangles and deadlocks. From these years, too,
dated the concept that instead of 'one world' there were
now to be two: a western world, led by and largely dependent upon the United States, and an eastern world,
dominated by the Soviet Union and permeated by communist ideology. As the peace treaties threw Poland
and most of the Balkans under Soviet economic and
political influence, as the American and British and
French zones of Germany were amalgamated economically, and as sharp divisions appeared within the United
Nations between the eastern and western blocs, this
picture of two rival worlds seemed to emerge ever more
luridly. Plans for a general peace settlement comparable
with that of 1919 were tacitly dropped, and each bloc
followed a policy guided by fear of its rival. No concession was made which would strengthen the strategic
or political defences of the other. By 1948 the world
scene had been transformed from one of embryonic
unity, under a concert of the major world powers, to
one of world schism making for a third world war.
History knows no more sudden transformation on so
vast and momentous a scale.

What were the chief components in this new balance
of power? The upheavals of war had made possible a
resumption of communist expansion, checked since
1919.[1] By 1948, the frontiers of the communist world
came as far westwards as the Russian zone of Germany
(Saxony) and Czechoslovakia (after the Communist
coup of February 1948), and as far eastwards as the

[1] See above, Chapter III, §1.

island of Sakhalin in Japan and northern Korea. The Soviet Union dropped an 'iron curtain' from Stettin in the Baltic to the head of the Adriatic sea, and correspondents from the west were virtually forbidden entry. In addition, the movements of resistance had produced strong Communist parties in the countries of western Europe. Even in France, in 1946, some 5,475,000 French men and women had voted for the Communists; and in Italy in the same year the party polled 4,358,000 votes. In each country the party participated in government until May 1947 and in each it enjoyed great influence over organized labour. But in sharp contrast to this, the Communist Party lost votes and seats in British elections until it had no parliamentary representatives and very slight influence over organized labour. It similarly lost ground in Belgium, the Netherlands, and Scandinavia, and in Latin America by 1950. In September 1947 the Cominform, or Communist Bureau of Information, was formed to replace the Comintern which had been formally dissolved in 1943. The great prestige which the sacrifices and victories of the Red Army had gained in the west during the war had, by 1948, been largely replaced by popular fears of Soviet imperialism. Within the countries of eastern Europe, the Soviet Union replaced Germany as the senior economic partner. Under its direction they planned for a more balanced economy and so aimed to expand heavy industries and improve agricultural methods. Collectivization of the land and group farming replaced the old system of landlord and peasant: and despite the failure or perversion of some of the plans, such concerted economic reorganization for the region of the Danube valley marked a new phase in the history of that long disturbed and impoverished area.

But Russian industrial capacity had been seriously injured by the war, whereas that of the United States had increased by half, and her agricultural output raised by 36 per cent. Because of the great increases in American national income and purchasing power, she was now the chief world supplier of capital goods and investment funds, and a coveted market for world exports. If Russian territorial expansion was great, American economic expansion was greater. She was the main factor in sustaining world economy, and by a vast scheme of foreign aid, investments, loans, and exports she became, even more than after 1920, the mainstay of economic recovery and prosperity in western Europe. On the other hand, such economic recovery was severely handicapped by an irresistible process of inflation.[1] And the economic strength of the non-communist world was diminished by grievous shortages, unstable trade relations, acute currency difficulties, and labour unrest which even the operations of new social security measures did not altogether allay.

The most striking consequence of the new balance and tension between the communist and non-communist worlds was the dramatic reversal of allied policy towards Germany. It also held the most profound implications for the future of Europe. For roughly two years the policy agreed upon by the allies at Potsdam in 1945 was carried out. It involved the zonal occupa-

[1] See further below, Chapter VI, §2.

tion of Germany, disarmament and demilitarization, 'denazification' of German life, the trial of war criminals, the decentralization of government and of economic organization, the dismantling of war-production plant and the exaction of reparations. In general, it was the policy consequent upon 'unconditional surrender' and fear of a resurgence of Hitlerism. But by 1950 the three western zones had been amalgamated, the new Bonn constitution was working, loans and other funds were being poured into western Germany for assisting in economic recovery, plans were afoot to re-arm Germany for defence against the Soviet Union, and before long Herr Krupp of Essen was to have the bulk of his fortune restored to him whilst alleged war criminals were freed and the sinister rumblings of re-formed Nazi movements could be heard. The economic and political recovery of Germany was the earliest consequence of the growing schism between east and west.

The British Commonwealth emerged from the war to find that its economic position in the world had also been revolutionized. Before the war the Commonwealth had 30 per cent. of the world's tonnage of shipping, now it had only 23 per cent. The United Kingdom, which had drawn a quarter of its foreign receipts from the £4,000,000,000 invested overseas, had by the end of the war sold £1,118,000,000 of its overseas capital holdings, and its income from this source was down to less than £100,000,000 a year. Having had to devote nearly three-quarters of its resources to the war effort, the United Kingdom had been transformed from a creditor to a debtor nation, with members of the

Commonwealth as its chief creditors. In 1946 it negotiated from the United States a loan of $3,750,000,000,
to be repaid in 50 years at 2 per cent. interest. Before
the war 63 per cent. of its foreign receipts had come
from exports, especially of coal, iron, steel, chemicals,
machinery, and textiles. Now its exports were down to
41 per cent. of their pre-war level, and many old markets were lost.

The political structure of the Commonwealth was
also transformed by the war. In 1948 Ceylon became a
Dominion but Burma proclaimed her complete independence and left the Commonwealth. In February
1947 Mr. Attlee announced that Britain would withdraw from India 'by a date not later than June 1948',
and as a result two new states of India and Pakistan
emerged. Pakistan chose Dominion status, and the new
Republic of India remained a member of the Commonwealth without allegiance to the monarchy. Britain's
similar withdrawal from her position as mandatory
power in Palestine made possible the new state of
Israel in 1948. Preparations were made for greater self-
government in some of the African colonies, especially
Nigeria and the Gold Coast. The Commonwealth now
rested more completely on faith in the cohesive value
of liberty: and it was committed to the experiment of
inspiring, in the great nations of coloured men, the
same loyalty and co-operative spirit which had been
nurtured by the evolution of self-government in the
white Dominions.

Other western European nations seemed to be also
in process of severing or of loosening the links which

tied them to the Far East. By 1949 Indonesia gained independence, whilst remaining linked somewhat tenuously to the crown of the Netherlands. From 1946 onwards war raged between the French and the movement of Viet-Minh in Indo-China. In Malaya British forces had to meet guerilla fighters. At the same time, between 1946 and 1948, the withdrawal of the Japanese from China precipitated civil war between Nationalists and Communists, which culminated by October 1949 in the proclamation of the Peoples' Republic of China under the Communist leader, General Mao Tse-tung. Now the country with the largest population in the world was thrown, apparently, into the Communist camp.

A new balance of power in the world seemed to result from all these momentous changes. In Europe a certain equilibrium had been struck between the power of western democracy, backed by United States economic and military aid, and the power of communism consolidated behind the iron curtain but extending far into the west through the strong Communist parties of western Europe. In the Far East the western European nations, including the British Commonwealth, were in retreat, whereas the power of both communism and the United States was expanded. United States forces remained in occupation of Japan and of most strategic islands in the Pacific. Russia had won a great new ally in China, and communist-aided forces were active in Indonesia, Indo-China, and Malaya. It seemed that the whole globe was well on the way to a partition between two rival camps, each intensely and aggressively hostile

O

to the other. Hostilities were already breaking out sporadically along the fringes—in the Soviet blockade of Berlin which was defeated by the remarkable effort of the Anglo-American airlift; in Persia, where the expulsion of Anglo-Iranian interests by Persian nationalists for a time opened the door to Soviet pressures; in Malaya, Indo-China and (after 1950) in Korea. If China had indeed replaced Japan as the aggressive power in the Pacific, and Russia had replaced Germany as the aggressor in Europe, then a general conflagration might be expected to follow sooner or later.

But this picture was greatly over-simplified, and the prospect was somewhat less gloomy than so pessimistic a view of the world scene might suggest. The capacity (and perhaps even the will) of each of the great new super-powers, the Soviet Union and the American Union, to dominate its allies and dependents was by no means complete. The British Commonwealth, still very vast and very cohesive in spite of its losses and perhaps because of its more liberal structure, was by no means subservient in its policy to United States interests. It persisted in following an independent policy in its recognition of the new Chinese government, in its handling of the Persian dispute, and in its commercial policy. France continued to fight the war in Indo-China, even when it was condemned abroad as an old-fashioned and imperialistic war, until it came to be widely regarded as a part of the general resistance to Communist expansion and even worthy of direct American economic aid. Within the Communist orbit, Marshal Tito of

Yugoslavia early asserted his independence, withstood severe Russian pressure, and became one of the greatest thorns in the side of Soviet power in the Balkans. It was by no means certain that Mao of China would follow directives issued from the Kremlin, and outbreaks of open unrest throughout all the Balkan countries, and in eastern Germany, were soon to show that other countries, too, were not reconciled to automatic subservience to their Russian protector. Everywhere, in short, separate nationalist interests were increasingly asserted, as against the notion of even hemispherical solidarity. India emerged as a great new Asiatic power, socialistic in the western tradition rather than communistic in the eastern. Warm cross-currents soon melted away the apparent freezing of the world into rival blocs.

If the world of 1950 was no nearer the unification and interdependence of which men had spoken and dreamed since 1914, neither did it conform to the sharp division and dichotomy of which many spoke in 1948. The true picture was still one of a balance between forces of integration and disintegration, of interdependence and separatism. It still, as always, knew a great deal of poverty and tyranny; and if man's ability to exploit the earth's resources for his own welfare had greatly increased, so too had the opportunities and facilities for tyranny. It was neither one world nor two worlds, but many worlds, capable of forming themselves into infinitely new and surprising patterns and alignments, defying alike the simple diagnoses of economists and political scientists, of optimists and pessimists.

Chapter Six
MID-CENTURY MILESTONES

§1. *International Relations*

BY the middle of the century it had become clear that
defeat of the common enemies had removed from the
victorious alliance of the United Nations its essential
bonds of unity. There was no longer an automatic harmony of purpose between the Soviet Union and the
west; and the temporary alliance for war was now replaced by intense mutual fears and distrust, in which
foundered the high hopes of making the United Nations a continuous and universal agency of world
organization to prevent war. This did not mean that
international relations reverted to anything like their
pre-war pattern. Apart from the revolution in the
balance of world power caused by the zonal division of
Germany and the occupation of Japan, the pressure of
economic necessities forged new links between the
United States, the Commonwealth, and the nations of
western Europe. The Charter of the United Nations
had provided for both separate action and regional co-
operation. Article 51 stipulated that 'Nothing in the
present Charter shall impair the inherent right of individual or collective self-defence if an armed attack
occurs against a member of the United Nations . . .'
and Article 52 that 'Nothing in the present Charter pre-
cludes the existence of regional arrangements or agencies
for dealing with such matters relating to the maintenance
of international peace and security as are appropriate for

regional action . . .' It was even laid down that 'The Security Council shall encourage the development of pacific settlement of local disputes through such regional arrangements or by such regional agencies...' The most striking feature of the world scene in 1950 was the proliferation of local or group organizations of this nature.

The two great international organizations of the inter-war years, the British Commonwealth of Nations and the Pan American organizations, not only remained in being but consolidated their cohesion. By remarkable ingenuity the formula was discovered which enabled India, though a republic, to remain within the framework of the Commonwealth and to accept the monarch as 'the symbol of the free association of its independent member nations and as such the Head of the Commonwealth'. The economic and administrative necessities of the new states of India and Pakistan led them to value such continued association with the Commonwealth, and ensured that their co-operation with the other members should become an active and far from nominal association. Although Gandhi was assassinated on 30 January 1948, and Mr. Jinnah died the following September, the successors—Mr. Nehru and Mr. Rajagopalachari in India, Mr. Khwaja Nazimuddin and Mr. Mohammad Ali in Pakistan—showed powers of statesmanship and leadership which augured well for the future. The defeat of General Smuts in the elections of May 1948, his replacement by Dr. Malan and the Nationalist party, and his death in 1950, robbed the Commonwealth of one of its wisest veteran statesmen and made the Union of South Africa one of the most explosive elements in the whole structure. The greatest problems of the Commonwealth remained those of Africa as a whole: but with that important exception there was no serious movement to disrupt its unity and its progress. Representatives from the Commonwealth countries met more frequently between the end of the war and 1950 than at any previous time in history,[1] and although it was clear that no unified foreign policy was possible, every other kind of co-operation was developed. One outstanding example was the Colombo Plan for technical assistance and concerted economic development in the countries of south-east Asia. Sponsored particularly by Australia, it prepared a six-year plan of development to bring more land under cultivation and irrigation, and to increase the sources of electrical power.

The American States held their ninth international conference at Bogota in 1948. They there drew up and signed a Charter of Organization for the twenty-one American Republics,[2] and so consolidated and integrated

---

[1] These include the Commonwealth Relations Conference (January 1944); Prime Ministers' Conference (May 1944); Commonwealth Conference at Canberra on the Japanese peace treaty and Pacific problems (April 1945); Prime Ministers' and Commonwealth Parliamentary Conferences (October 1948); Prime Ministers' Conference on India's membership (April 1949); Commonwealth Relations Conference (June 1949); Finance Ministers' Conference (July 1949); informal talks between Commonwealth trade unions leaders (September 1949); Commonwealth Foreign Ministers' Conference at Colombo (January 1950).

[2] The earlier Treaty of Rio de Janeiro, of September 1947, was not signed by Nicaragua or Ecuador: it embodied a real regional alliance for mutual self-defence, and was in effect implemented by the organization set up at Bogota.

the achievements and experience which had resulted from fifty years of active co-operation. It acknowledged the principle (Article 24) that 'Every act of aggression by a State against the territorial integrity or inviolability of the territory or against the sovereignty or political independence of an American State shall be considered as an act of aggression against the other American States'. It thus formulated expressly the principle which had long underlain, tacitly, the system of imperial defence in the Commonwealth.

These established systems were now joined by various new organizations, of which the most important was the North Atlantic Treaty Organization formed in April 1949. That it was not, and was not intended to be, a regional organization was emphasized by its formation under Article 51 of the United Nations Charter providing for individual or collective self-defence, rather than under Articles 52 or 53 providing for regional arrangements; and by the adherence to it of non-Atlantic states such as Italy, Turkey, and Greece. Its other members were, from the start, the United States, Canada, the United Kingdom, France, Belgium, Luxembourg, the Netherlands, Denmark, Norway, Iceland, and Portugal. It equipped itself with integrated military forces under centralized command and control, and the members agreed (Article 5) that 'an armed attack against one or more of them in Europe or North America shall be considered an attack against them all'. The North Atlantic Council, representative of all member governments, was the central political authority. Although its prime purpose was to prepare a coherent system of defence for the Atlantic, Europe, and the Mediterranean, its activities were extended to include economic and financial affairs.

§2. *World Economy*

The next most impressive step towards solid international co-operation was the movement towards the economic integration of the western European nations. It had its beginnings in 1944 in the formation of the close customs union between Belgium, Luxembourg, and the Netherlands which came to be known as 'Benelux': and the three states increasingly acted, for purposes of international agreements, as one unit. In March 1948 these three countries signed, with France and the United Kingdom, the Brussels Treaty of Economic, Social and Cultural Collaboration and Collective Self-Defence. It set up a joint military organization for common defence, known as Uniforce, which was later absorbed into the North Atlantic Treaty Organization. In June 1947 the United States Secretary of State, General George C. Marshall, announced a plan for the economic rehabilitation of Europe and promised extensive American aid if the European nations would unite for the purpose. The Marshall Plan gave rise to a series of European bodies for organizing the distribution of American aid, and in particular the Organization for European Economic Co-operation (O.E.E.C.), set up in April 1948. These were all essentially intergovernmental bodies. In 1949 and 1950 two new types of international bodies were envisaged. One, the Council of Europe, with the aim of achieving 'greater unity between its members for the purpose of safeguarding and realizing the ideals and principles which are their common heritage and facilitating their economic and social progress', combined a Committee of Ministers, representing the governments of all members, with a Consultative Assembly composed of representatives of political parties and individuals chosen by governments. It produced little concrete result. The other was the European Coal and Steel Community, derived from proposals of the French Foreign Minister, M. Robert Schuman, in May 1950. The aim of the Community was to pool the coal, iron, and steel production of member countries, to establish a single market in these commodities, to promote economic expansion and full employment, and to raise the standard of living. It was to be organized under a supranational authority. Great Britain held aloof from membership, but the three Benelux countries, France, Italy, and western Germany proceeded to set up such a body.

It was already clear, by the end of 1950, that the countries of western Europe would be confronted with a choice of two different principles of co-operation. One, building on the projects of the Council of Europe and the concepts of the Schuman proposal, would involve a federalist solutior of European problems; the other, following the more traditional pattern, would mean that international relations would remain essentially a matter for co-operation between national governments. And it was already clear that Great Britain, speaking through both her main political

parties, would co-operate fully in European affairs but
would not, because of her position as the hinge of the
sterling area and of the Commonwealth, participate in
federalist organizations which would involve merging
either her economy or her armed forces into a common
pool.[1]

Yet another form of international grouping which
came into existence by 1945 was the Arab League, including the seven Arab states of Egypt, Saudi Arabia,
Iraq, Syria, Lebanon, Transjordan, and Yemen. This
banding together of the Arab states was in part a consequence of war-time experience of the Middle East
Supply Centre. It was originally a British but latterly
an Anglo-American organization for co-ordinating the
supplies, transport, and needs of the whole area of the
Middle East, an area vital to the allied effort because of
its rich oil resources and because strategically it strad-
dled world air routes. It had the effect of stimulating
intercommunication between the Arab countries and
accustomed them to thinking of their common problems on a regional basis. The League was also partly
the result of common hostility towards the Jewish
Zionist movement. When Israel proclaimed itself a
sovereign state in May 1948 and as the British withdrew their forces from Palestine, that country was invaded by forces from Syria, Lebanon, Transjordan,
Iraq, and Egypt. Warfare continued until January 1949,

[1] The proposals for a European Defence Community, with
a unified military force, followed soon after but fall outside
the period covered by this book. The sterling area, by 1950,
included all the Commonwealth (except Canada), Iceland,
Iraq, and the Faroes, and comprised some 540 million people.

and resulted in the defeat of the Arab states. By 1950 the new state of Israel had been officially recognized by most countries in the world, though not by her nearest neighbours, the Arab states. Despite these reverses the Arab League continued to develop co-operation amongst its members. In June 1950 all except Iraq and Transjordan (both under the ancient House of Hashim) signed a collective security pact covering economic matters as well as political and military. The League evolved economic and cultural commissions. But it remained as much a field for internal Arab rivalries as an expression of unity; and the peoples of this area, enjoying greater political independence than those of the colonial territories but sharing in their backward and dependent economic status, constituted a special world problem. Although unlikely to become politically more than a very loose confederation, the Arab League formed in the world of 1950 an important power bloc, unpredictable in action because of its internal divisions between Egypt, Saudi Arabia, and Lebanon on one side, and Iraq and Transjordan on the other.

The international scene, halfway through the twentieth century, had therefore several clear features. One was a remarkable proliferation of diverse forms of international co-operation: some continental, like the Organization of American States, some multi-continental, like the Commonwealth; some virtually universal, like the functional organizations of the United Nations, others regional, like the Arab League; some primarily for mutual defence and security, like N.A.T.O., others for the vaguest kind of international discussion, like the Strasbourg Assembly of the Council of Europe.

A second feature was the hegemony of the United States in the world. From being a power anxious to keep out of foreign entanglements, especially in Europe, the United States had become a leader of world movements, a source of financial and economic aid vital to the recovery and prosperity of much of the rest of the world, and the possessor of the most devastating weapons of destruction ever known to mankind. Her relative inexperience in this world role, and the world's unfamiliarity with her modes of behaviour in international relations, were themselves important elements in the world situation. Her initiative in ensuring military action in Korea in June 1950 on behalf of the South Korean government opened a new chapter in the history of international enforcement of United Nations decisions.

A third feature was the condition of world tension and fear known as 'the cold war'. The label was not completely appropriate, for there had already been after 1945 actual operations of war in Greece, Palestine, Indo-China, Malaya, Kashmir, as well as in Korea. But at least the world was still at war in the sense described by Thomas Hobbes:

'For "war" consisteth not in battle only, or the act of fighting; but in a tract of time wherein the will to contend by battle is sufficiently known . . . For as the nature of foul weather lieth not in a shower of rain, but in an inclination thereto of many days together, so the nature of war consisteth not in actual fighting, but in the known disposition thereto all the time there is no assurance to the contrary.'

So the modern 'Leviathans' maintained peacetime conscription and enormous expenditure on armaments: and not only was much of the international co-operation prompted by fears for security, but the flow of economic and technical aid was prompted by anxiety to remove social conditions favourable for the spread of communism as well as by more altruistic and humanitarian motives.

§3. *Diffusion of Welfare*

The population of the world increased by some 175 millions during the decade between 1937 and 1947. Even without the destruction and dislocation of a world war, there would thus have been very much greater pressure on the world's supply of food by the middle of the century, unless this increase had been accompanied by a veritable revolution in agricultural production. In 1937 the League of Nations recorded that not less than half the world's population suffered from malnutrition. Perhaps this had always been so: but with a tendency for the numbers of mankind to increase at the rate of roughly another 25 million each year, one of the world's most urgent economic problems in 1950 was to increase the production and improve the distribution of food.

By 1950, the Food and Agriculture Organization calculated that the production of food (excluding fish) was distributed in the world as follows, whilst the population was distributed as in the second column:

Region	Percentage of food production	Percentage of population
Far East	32.0	54.5
Europe	23.5	18.0
Near East	4.4	5.5
Africa	4.7	7.0
Latin America	10.0	7.0
U.S.A.-Canada	22.6	7.5
Oceania	2.8	.5
	100.0	100.0

Thus the greater half of mankind, which lived in the Far East, produced less than one-third of the world's food: whereas North America, with only 7.5 per cent. of the world's mouths to feed, grew more than one-fifth of the world's food. This is the economic background to the international hegemony of the United States.

It is one of the unobserved blessings of mankind that during the fifteen years after 1937 climatic conditions in North America were favourable to good crops, and the world was spared the series of semi-droughts which, in the middle nineteen-thirties, caused an average fall in production of over 30 per cent. per acre. Recurrence of such conditions during the years of war and post-war scarcities would have brought immeasurable suffering to humanity. The problems of growing more food by means of increasing cultivated areas and yields, by improved irrigation, pest control, and technical knowledge, were tackled more vigorously by governments and by such international agencies as the Food and

Agriculture Organization, the World Health Organization, and U.N.E.S.C.O. Particularly in the Far East, research and the spread of improved techniques and technical aid were likely to yield considerable improvement in the world's most distressed regions.

Problems of distribution were no less important than problems of greater production. So uneven a natural distribution of food supplies would matter less if international trade could effectively distribute them. But when the areas most in need of food are the least developed economically, and international trade is dislocated by war and debts and obstructed by tariffs and other protective devices, there are formidable impediments to redistribution. In 1950 the chief food-importing countries in Europe were the United Kingdom, Germany, Italy, Belgium, and Switzerland; and in the Far East, Japan, Ceylon, and Malaya. The European countries were particularly dependent on imports of certain foodstuffs, such as fats, cereals, sugar, and meat. The Far Eastern countries, including India, though not dependent on imports for the bulk of their food, depended on vital marginal supplies without which they were liable to suffer local famine. In these ways the interdependence of the continents was not only greater than ever before, but was more widely and fully appreciated.

The world-wide tendency to inflation after the war, already noted, had its roots in world economic conditions beyond the control of any one government. In 1948 the United Nations Economic Report analysed the reasons for this inflationary trend:

In most countries, the inflationary pressures may be attributed on the one hand to the pressure of demand generated by budget deficits, or large net exports, or high rates of private investment, or spending of accumulated liquid assets, and on the other hand, to the scarce supplies of consumer goods. This situation has caused a rise in prices which tends to adjust the demand for consumption goods to the supply by raising profits to the point where the savings resulting from these profits are sufficient to finance the increased investment and government deficits. In the process the relative share of wages in the national income falls and the necessaries of life tend to be distributed very inequitably. The resulting efforts by workers to prevent deterioration in their position by wage increases are frustrated by subsequent price increases, and thus the inflationary spiral develops.[1]

Governments could, however, redress the inequitable distribution of necessities by all the devices of the 'welfare state': by food subsidies, as in Britain, by a system of lavish family allowances, as in France, and by graded taxation, as in most European countries. But because so much of the essential imports of food had to come from the United States and Canada, countries of the sterling area found themselves faced with a large dollar deficit.

Before the war world trade had often been triangular in character. Latin American countries paid for their imports from the United States by their export surplus to Europe: and the countries of the Far East paid for their imports from Europe with their large exports of

[1] *Salient Features in the World Economic Situation, 1945–47*: Economic Report, Department of Economic Affairs, United Nations, January 1948: pp. 24–25.

raw materials to the United States. In this way the European economy had become the centre of a wider international exchange of goods and services. The war demolished this pattern. Because of currency difficulties a network of bilateral barter agreements contrived to eliminate currency as a means of payment. The partition of Europe by the iron curtain helped to change the whole orientation of European economy. Before the war the industrialized countries of western Europe, including Germany, had accounted for almost half the world's industrial production, and much of their trade was with eastern Europe in return for foodstuffs and raw materials.[1] The countries of Europe, to a much greater degree than those of any other continent, were dependent upon international trade. Those in eastern Europe were heavily dependent on the countries of western Europe, especially Germany and the United Kingdom, for both their industrial imports and their markets: and almost half their imports were manufactured goods. Immediately after the war these countries traded much more with the Soviet Union, although within a few years their trading connexions with western Europe were revived. Meanwhile the western countries lost much of their trade with Asia and Latin America, and vastly increased their trade with the United States. Thus the political cleavage in Europe had its counterpart in an economic reorientation, the eastern nations looking more eastwards, the western looking more westwards.

[1] Apart from the United Kingdom, the western countries in 1935 drew 58 per cent. of their imports from eastern Europe, which took 69 per cent. of their exports.

P

But both in Asia and in Latin America, political difficulties impeded smooth commercial relations. Latin America, whose trade with Europe virtually stopped during the early years of the war, established new commercial relations with the United States until, in 1945, it was taking 39 per cent. of United States exports and was sending half its own exports to the United States. Similarly cut off from rice supplies from Asia, it so increased its own production that it not only became self-sufficient but had a surplus for export. Several Latin American states evolved long-term plans, often under governmental direction or control, for economic development.

European relations with Africa were diversely affected by the war. That continent includes most of the non-self-governing territories administered by the western European powers, and 80 per cent. of its exports normally went to Europe whilst two-thirds of its imports came from Europe. In general, the war led to deterioration in the French territories after the fall of France in 1940, and North Africa experienced actual war-damage; whereas the British territories benefited from the increased demand for their valuable exports. The Union of South Africa, in particular, almost extinguished its external debt and because of its gold resources acquired enhanced advantages in world trade. The Belgian Congo, like Northern Rhodesia, prospered from the world demand for non-ferrous metals. But Africa as a whole suffered, like the rest of the world, from inflationary trends, often intensified by poor crops and shortages of capital equipment. Both France and Britain instituted long-term development plans for their colonial territories, involving heavy capital investments and an expansion of technical facilities.

.   .   .   .   .

The main economic consequence of the intensification of international fears during the post-war years of reconstruction was that most countries were confronted with the dilemma which had been described, before the war, as the choice of 'guns or butter'. The world food shortage, the disruption of international trade, the development of the 'welfare state' and the spread of democratic socialism all dictated that material and human resources be directed to production for prosperity. The fears of a third world war dictated that a large part of national resources be devoted to security: that manpower needed for production be diverted to the armed forces, that capital equipment needed for industrial and agricultural development be devoted to rearmament, that money be spent on swords rather than ploughshares. But this dilemma affected different nations in different ways. In those countries whose industrial capacity had been greatly expanded during the war, particularly the United States, programmes of rearmament held certain economic advantages. They ensured full employment during years when an economic depression might otherwise have set in. In those countries whose economies had been adversely affected by the war, such as the United Kingdom and most western European countries, the double burden of expenditure on social services and rearmament imposed a very severe strain. They were thus confronted with the further political dilemma, that unless they maintained social services at a high enough level to prevent real social distress, they might breed communism internally by their very efforts to check its expansion internationally. This dilemma was felt particularly in countries such as France and Italy, with strong internal communist movements: and they happened also to be the countries most exposed, internationally, to any western aggressions of Soviet power. In the United Kingdom, where the sharp decline of the Communist party removed any fears of internal communism, the dilemma was more social than political. Her labour force was barely sufficient to maintain the standard of living of a population whose age-structure was becoming increasingly top-heavy. With the post-war decline in her international position, she had no slack of surplus production to be absorbed by rearmament, such as existed in the United States; and from the outset every diversion of resources to rearmament meant inroads on social services, housing, and schools, new demands for 'austerity' and a tightening of the belt, continuation of a crushing burden of taxation.

Thus in all European nations international tensions meant, in some form, profound internal tensions too. They meant economic impoverishment at a time of urgent economic reconstruction, except in so far as generous United States aid and loans offered some relief. This impeded the defence of western Europe and in France, further drained by the long war in Indo-China and with a very weak fiscal system and unstable governments, it became virtually impossible to balance the budget. The ultimate dilemma of the world economy, in 1950, was how it could be used to provide both social security and military security at the same time: or, to use the words of President Roosevelt, how both freedom from want and freedom from fear could be achieved simultaneously.

The century before 1914 saw an almost continuous process of European expansion: by emigration and the diffusion of European culture, by the growth of international trade and oversea investment, by the concentration of military and economic power in the hands of the European nations, by their establishment of control over undeveloped areas in Asia and Africa. One theme of world history after 1914 was the contraction of Europe. The predominance of the United States in 1919 and the importance of the Soviet Union in international affairs between the wars were omens of a tendency which became pefectly clear only after 1945. Now Europe was divided into orbits of great-power influence. Its economy was impoverished by warfare and much of its overseas assets liquidated. Movements for self-government and separation seethed in most of its colonial territories. Europe was clearly no longer the centre of gravity of wealth and power in the world. More than a century earlier perceptive and prophetic observers like Alexis de Tocqueville and Alexander Herzen had predicted not only the decline of Europe but also the rise to pre-eminence of the United States and Russia. In 1921 General Smuts had been premature but prophetic in proclaiming Europe to be 'no longer of the first importance'. By 1950 it was reasonable to speculate whether this decline of Europe was permanent, and whether the continent which for 2,000 years had been a fountain of civilization and progress had now exhausted itself. If so, the period 1914–1950 was indeed one of the millennial and catastrophic eras in human history.

Without attempting to answer so momentous a riddle, it is possible to point out a few considerations which have bearing upon it. The first is that even the relative contraction of Europe in world importance in no way involved the end of European civilization. By the previous century of expansion all the essentials of European civilization had been spread throughout the other continents of the world. Latin America absorbed much of the culture and civilization of Latin Europe, and the Dominions of the British Commonwealth were populated by men who inherited much that was best in British ways of life. The United States had been composed of the overflow from Europe and was itself an heir of European civilization. The Soviet Union, despite the ideological and political barriers which had grown up to divide it from Europe, had adopted and adapted the technologies and many of the ideas generated in Europe. The fruits of European civilization, like men of European stock, had been too widely dispersed over the face of the earth for them to be extinguished.

There remains the further and different question, whether the springs of culture and civilization within Europe itself had dried up. Were the rich diversity of cultures, the inventive genius which had given birth to modern science and technology, the accumulated wisdom and skills which had made possible twentieth-century organization and administration, at last becoming exhausted? This riddle time alone could answer. But at least so far as western Europe was concerned, there seemed no good reason to be pessimistic in 1950. The conception of using all material resources and human skill in organization for the widest possible diffusion of welfare was itself a conception originating in western Europe: and that conception in 1950 was coming to dominate the world. Many age-long afflictions of mankind had been brought within the category of remediable ills: such afflictions as plagues and famines, destitution and squalor, ignorance and premature death. Within a hundred years western man had added a full generation to the average length of life: and he was now making strenuous efforts to extend such blessings to areas of the world hitherto less fortunate. It was likely that the populations of developed countries would continue to increase for some decades to come, because of the fall in infant mortality and the increase in the expectancy of life. Largely because of medical skills and facilities imported from the western nations, the less developed areas of the world, too, showed a fall in their death-rates which was more rapid than any decline in birth-rates.

No less important, there had grown up along with this material progress a wider and more generous conception of human justice. Within the western nations all the social security measures and the devices of the welfare state were succeeding in achieving a more just distribution of the necessaries of life among their peoples as a whole. Although much remained to be done, it was undeniable that public education and old age pensions, social insurance and schemes for full employment, health services and redistributive systems of taxation, made longer life more worth while for the mass of Europeans. Colonial imperialism had long shaken off its more ruthless and exploiting characteristics, and there were genuine impulses to find in principles of trusteeship and greater self-government, even in racial partnership, a new basis for relations between the developed and under-developed nations of the world. Not only were such principles embodied in the Charter of the United Nations to which most of the world had subscribed but even more significantly the leading colonial powers had begun to apply them to the government of their overseas territories not held formally under United Nations trusteeship.[1] The Dutch in Indonesia, the French in North Africa and Indo-China, the British in Africa, were all making firm moves towards recognition of the political and social rights of colonial peoples. That these moves were not always made as fast as the most politically conscious nationalist leaders of these peoples wished, and were at times made only under the compulsion of political necessities, were less cause for surprise than the fact

[1] Cf. Chapter XI of the Charter, regarding all non-self-governing territories, which enunciates the principle that 'the interests of the inhabitants of these territories are paramount.'

that the 'colonial revolution', for it was no less than
that, had become so universal and immediate a feature
of world history.

.   .   .   .   .

This colonial revolution, which in its earliest form
goes back at least to the Indian Mutiny of 1857, dates
continuously from the Boxer rebellion in China in 1900
and the victory of Japan over Russia in 1905. It was
brought to its first great climax by Japanese conquests
in Asia and the Pacific in the second world war. Eman-
cipation of Asia from the white race was then loudly
proclaimed, and was brought within measurable dis-
tance of achievement. The demand for greater racial
equality, both political and economic, was fast bringing
to an end the nineteenth-century equation between
racial differences and economic status. The peoples of
Asia and Africa were quick to learn the lesson—and not
only from Soviet propaganda—that the means to material progress and greater equality are industrialization.
In no other way can the standard of living be raised,
and the necessaries of life produced in more adequate
quantities and distributed more equitably. This was
the principle underlying the great changes taking place
in India and Pakistan, China and Africa. It was simply
the extended application of techniques and principles
learnt from Europe and America. With these principles
and techniques spread the characteristically European
ideals of national self-determination and unification, of
democracy and social welfare. As in nineteenth-century Europe, the simultaneous ferment of democratic

political ideas and industrial techniques produced a remarkable revolutionary ferment throughout the 200 million inhabitants of the less developed areas of the world. Domination by European powers was approaching its end. Future relations would be either those of partnership and good-neighbourliness, or they would be those of war.

This revolution, too, was intricately connected with the tension between communism and the west, in part because the Soviet Union encouraged and exploited the colonial difficulties of its rivals and in part because colonial nationalist movements tended to adopt the principles of socialism or communism rather than those of liberalism which they had come to identify with white superiority and control. It was thus a feature of the world in 1950 that colonial uprisings in Malaya and Indo-China, as in parts of Africa, became confused with the wider conflict between communism and the democracies; just as United States opinion, with traditional sentiments strongly hostile to colonial powers, was confused by finding itself in some agreement with Soviet attitudes towards colonial independence.

As in 1914, there were signs that the British Commonwealth was in some respects better fitted to adapt itself to the new colonial situation than was France.[1]

---

[1] Cf. above, Chapter I, §1. The French policy, of bringing colonial peoples into increasingly closer 'association' with France, had once been a novel and hopeful one: but with the current tendency towards nationalist separatism it seemed, by 1950, to be less in tune with the aspirations of the colonial world.

The completeness of Britain's concession of independence to India, Pakistan, Burma, and Ceylon left a deep impression in Asia. Its prompt establishment of institutions for greater self-government in Nigeria, the Gold Coast, and the West Indies showed that it meant to follow a systematic policy of liberalization. Its plans for colonial welfare and development showed some appreciation of the economic aspirations of the colonies, and the desirability of further industrialization. Schemes for grouping smaller areas into larger and more viable federations or units were devised: giving rise to the Malayan Union of 1948, the Federation of the West Indies, the regional organizations for consultation and co-operation in West Africa and East Africa, and the controversial project for a federation of Northern and Southern Rhodesia with Nyasaland. In all, the Commonwealth showed the qualities of ingenuity, flexibility, and adaptability which normally make for survival and development. The French Union, devised in 1946 to give the French overseas territories greater representation in both the French Parliament and in a consultative assembly of its own, was less in accord with colonial desires for greater self-government and independence. Indeed the Brazzaville Conference of 1944, attended not by native officials but by colonial administrators, declared that 'the formation of independent governments in the colonies, however far off, cannot be contemplated'. Nevertheless, by the constitution of 1946 and subsequent legislation, the principles of racial equality were stated, local representative assemblies were set up, and effort was made to reach some compromise between the old concept of colonial empire and current aspirations for responsible self-government.

There was a certain parallel between this great colonial revolution and the development of the welfare state internally. Both represented that fusion of nationalistic and socialistic ideals which the Charter of Philadelphia of 1944, already mentioned, summed up in the words: 'all human beings, irrespective of race, creed or sex, have the right to pursue both their material well-being and their spiritual development in conditions of freedom and dignity, of economic security and equal opportunity'. Here was a universalist ethic which at least chimed with an increasingly interdependent world. It was matched, in western Europe, by the predominance after the war of socialistic parties which, whilst retaining their distinct national characteristics and aspirations, nevertheless shared common ideals and purposes. Nor were these only the traditional social-democratic parties of the west. In France, Italy, and Germany they significantly included powerful parties of Christian Democrats, representing a synthesis of forces which had hitherto been mutually hostile. These parties, which between them attracted the support of more than 25 million western European voters, denoted a new degree of fusion between the forces of republicanism and socialism on one side, and the forces of Roman Catholicism on the other. Led by statesmen of the ability and vigour of M. Schuman, Signor de Gasperi, and Dr. Adenauer, they played a particularly important part in the movements for the economic and political integration of western Europe already noted.[1]

Despite the territorial contraction of Europe by 1950, and its decline in world power and importance relative to other continents, there seemed no grounds for assuming that its capacities for progressive leadership were exhausted. What happened in Europe was still of immense and immediate importance everywhere else in the world. The test of its potentialities lay in the ability of its national leaders to adapt themselves to a new situation. Their control over the destinies of their countries was no longer so independent. They were obliged to work in closer relation with the leaders of the great non-European powers: and these included not only the United States and the Soviet Union, but India and China. They were also obliged to find a new basis for collaboration with the leaders of the colonial territories. But these inescapable conditions for European statecraft did not in themselves diminish the decisive importance of continental Europe in world affairs. It might be maintained that just as in the nineteenth century the historic Turkish Empire was 'the sick man of Europe', so in the twentieth Europe had become 'the sick man of the world'. But the analogy with Turkey might be extended: and just as Turkey of the inter-war years, contracted and of diminished world importance,

[1] See above, §1. It may be noted that the Constitutions of France (1946), Italy (1948) and Western Germany (1949), in all of which Christian Democratic parties had a formative share, included specific provisions for the limitation of national sovereignty in the cause of international order and security. The moves towards federalism in western Europe were made possible by the coincidence in power of the three leaders named.

found new cohesion and fresh springs of development, so too might the compressed and weakened Europe of 1950. Its very contraction might become a source of new strength. But the indispensable conditions for its success were a great increase in productivity and avoidance of a third world war. Without these conditions, the great social transformation involved in a more even diffusion of wealth and welfare as between different nations in Europe, as between the different continents of the world, and as between different social classes within each community, would be quite unattainable.

.   .   .   .   .

As was mentioned in the Foreword, it has been no purpose of this book to propose solutions to the problems posed by the last generation of world history. The account of world events in these years has been made as meaningful as the trend of events themselves seemed to justify. But if there is any moral to be drawn from the trend of events it is perhaps not that they follow any clear or predictable pattern, nor that there appears to be any inevitable movement towards sharp dichotomies or simple antitheses. It is rather that no one nation or group of nations or continent finds it possible to control events as it would like; that the most concerted international efforts more often surprise their participants by their unforeseen consequences than they achieve precisely what anyone intended. The ultimate destination of present trends remains unknown. The three greatest power-units in the world of 1950 were the United States, the Commonwealth, and the

Soviet Union. All are multi-national. Does this betoken that the age of the nation-state as the normal unit of diplomacy and world relationships is coming to an end? Or does it portend the growth of a wider sense of nationalism, more comprehensive in its reach and incalculably momentous in its consequences? Has mankind any freedom to choose? The attitude prompted by the study of recent world history should be humility rather than pride. It is rare for men to extract from great events just the benefits which they hope for. And some of the most perplexing predicaments of mankind are settled more by the pressure of necessities which impose reluctant concessions on either side than by the most ingenious blue-prints of experts or prophets.

BIBLIOGRAPHICAL NOTE

THE following bibliographical note makes no attempt
to do more than to mention some fifty books which the
reader will find of use should he wish to pursue further
the main topics of inter-continental and international
relations discussed above. Throughout he will find
a good atlas indispensable. No attempt has been made
to list books dealing with the internal history of different nations, but in general enough information about
internal developments will usually be found to be contained in the books mentioned to make clear their significance for world history. Books in languages other than
English, however relevant and valuable, have been
omitted from the list unless an English translation
exists.

A. GENERAL:

Probably the most useful general and comprehensive
history of the period is F. P. Chambers, C. P. Harris
and C. C. Bayley: *This Age of Conflict: A Contemporary
World History 1914 to the Present* (London, rev. ed.
1950): but the forthcoming twelfth volume of the new
Cambridge Modern History will deal with the period
from 1900 on lines more similar to those suggested in
this book.

Every student of recent international affairs owes a
debt to the stimulating study by E. H. Carr: *The
Twenty Years' Crisis, 1919-1939: An Introduction to
the Study of International Relations* (London, 2nd ed.

1946). The same writer's *International Relations between the Two World Wars, 1919–1939* (London 1947) is a brilliant and brief survey of that period, which is covered at greater length in G. M. Gathorne-Hardy: *A Short History of International Affairs, 1920–1939* (Oxford: R.I.I.A. 3rd ed. 1942).

The military history of the two world wars is told in C. R. M. F. Cruttwell: *A History of the Great War, 1914–1918* (Oxford, 1936) and Cyril Falls: *The Second World War: A Short History* (London, 1948). Useful special studies of the revolutionary consequences of air power are Air Marshal Lord Tedder: *Air Power in War* (London, 1948) and H. E. Wimperis: *World Power and Atomic Energy: The Impact on International Relations* (London, 1946).

Economic aspects of recent world history are dealt with in A. Birnie: *Economic History of Europe, 1760–1930* (London, 1930) and A. L. Bowley: *Some Economic Consequences of the Great War* (London, Home University Library, 1930). A standard work on population is A. M. Carr-Saunders: *World Population: Past Growth and Present Trends* (Oxford, R.I.I.A., 1936), and a famous and challenging exploration of the cultural and social consequences of the growth of population is Ortega y Gasset: *The Revolt of the Masses* (Eng. trans. New York, 1932).

Amongst the many studies of international organization after 1919 are such personal accounts as Sir Harold Butler: *The Lost Peace: A Personal Impression* (London, 1941), Viscount Cecil: *A Great Experiment* (London, 1941) and Robert Dell: *The Geneva Racket (1920–*

Q

1939) (London, 1941). These books capture the atmosphere of Geneva and reveal the nature of international organization between the wars better than more academic studies. The most authoritative but somewhat large and technical study of the United Nations is L. M. Goodrich and E. Hambro: *Charter of the United Nations: commentary and documents* (London, 2nd ed. 1949). The documentary collection *United Nations Documents, 1941–1945* (London, 1946) published by the Royal Institute of International Affairs is indispensable material for studying international organizations after the second world war. C. H. Alexandrowicz: *International Economic Organizations* (London, 1952) is a valuable examination of the economic agencies throughout the whole period. The problems and the experience of making peace settlements after great wars are discussed in D. Thomson, E. Meyer, and A. Briggs: *Patterns of Peacemaking* (London, 1945).

The nature of nationalism and its consequences for world history are examined by A. Cobban: *National Self-Determination* (Oxford, R.I.I.A., 1945) and by E. H. Carr: *Nationalism and After* (London, 1945). The little book by C. B. Fawcett: *Frontiers* (Oxford, 1918) contains a stimulating discussion of the nature of political and geographical frontiers from a Great War standpoint. The problems of extending national self-government to colonial territories are considered in a provocative manner by W. R. Crocker: *Self-Government for the Colonies* (London, 1949), and there is a useful short survey of world colonial problems in Eric A. Walker: *Colonies* (Cambridge, 1944). The relations between nationalism and socialism are discussed in F. Borkenau: *Socialism: National or International* (London, 1942).

B. REGIONAL:

The structure and relations of the British Commonwealth of Nations may be conveniently studied in J. Coatman: *The British Family of Nations* (London, 1950) or in H. V. Hodson: *Twentieth Century Empire* (London, 1948). Nicholas Mansergh: *The Commonwealth and the Nations: Studies in British Commonwealth Relations* (London, R.I.I.A., 1948) is a collection of brief essays on some important aspects of the subject. British relations with the United States are discussed in Crane Brinton: *The United States and Britain* (Cambridge, Mass. rev. ed. 1948), and with the European countries between the wars in R. W. Seton-Watson: *Britain and the Dictators: A Survey of Post-War British Policy* (Cambridge, 1938).

The relations between the Soviet Union and the rest of the world cannot be appreciated without some knowledge of both the Bolshevik Revolution and the doctrines of Marxism. A knowledge of both may be gained, in brief, from C. Hill: *Lenin and the Russian Revolution* (London, 1947) and R. N. Carew Hunt: *The Theory and Practice of Communism: An Introduction* (London, 1950). Soviet foreign policy in general is exhaustively examined by Max Beloff: *The Foreign Policy of Soviet Russia, 1929–1941* (2 vols., Oxford, R.I.I.A., 1947–9), whilst relations with the United States in particular are dealt with by V. M. Dean: *The United States and Russia* (London, 1947). How Communism has spread in the world is examined in H. Seton-Watson: *The Pattern of Communist Revolution: A Historical Analysis* (London, 1953).

André Siegfried: *Europe's Crisis* (Eng. trans. London, 1935) is a lively short analysis, by a distinguished Frenchman, of the changing economic status of Europe in the world. Good regional studies of the continent are Elizabeth Monroe: *The Mediterranean in Politics* (London, 2nd ed. 1939), H. G. Wanklyn: *The Eastern Marchlands of Europe* (London, 1941), and H. Seton-Watson: *Eastern Europe between the Wars, 1918–1941* (Cambridge, 1945). The impact of Europe on Asia is well handled in a brief form by Sir John T. Pratt: *The Expansion of Europe in the Far East* (London, 1947).

United States policy in general is admirably described by D. Perkins: *The Evolution of American Foreign Policy* (New York, Home University Library, 1948), and more fully for this period by S. F. Bemis: *The United States as a World Power: A Diplomatic History, 1900–1950* (New York, 1950). On the recovery of the U.S.A. from the world economic crisis see D. W. Brogan: *Roosevelt and the New Deal* (London, 1952) and on its relations with Latin America in particular see the full treatment by S. F. Bemis: *The Latin American Policy of the United States: An Historical Interpretation* (New York, 1943). R. A. Humphreys: *The Evolution of Modern Latin America* (Oxford, 1946) is a convenient and authoritative treatment of the South American republics in modern times.

The reader wishing to know more about problems of the Pacific and the Far East can most profitably consult

Nathaniel Peffer: *Japan and the Pacific* (London, 1935), in many respects a prophetic book; and Sir J. T. Pratt: *War and Politics in China* (London, 1943). Percival Spear: *India, Pakistan and the West* (Oxford, Home University Library, 2nd ed. 1952) is a brief historical examination of Indian developments, which may be supplemented by A. Mellor: *India since Partition* (London, 1951) on more recent developments. V.W.W.S. Purcell: *The Chinese in Southeast Asia* (London, R.I.I.A., 1951) is a massive but indispensable account of that important problem. Pacific problems in general are usefully described by G. W. Keeton: *China, the Far East and the Future* (London, 1943).

Index

Printed by W. & J. Mackay & Co. Ltd., Chatham